AN INTERDISCIPLINARY APPROACH
TO ISSUES AND PRACTICES IN TEACHER EDUCATION

AN INTERDISCIPLINARY APPROACH
TO ISSUES AND PRACTICES IN TEACHER EDUCATION

Edited by
Gwendolyn M. Duhon Boudreaux

Mellen Studies in Education
Volume 38

The Edwin Mellen Press
Lewiston•Queenston•Lampeter

Library of Congress Cataloging-in-Publication Data

An interdisciplinary approach to issues and practices in teacher
education / edited by Gwendolyn M. Duhon Boudreaux.
   p. cm.-- (Mellen Studies in education ; v. 38)
   Includes bibliographical references.
   ISBN 0-7734-8246-6 (hard)
   1. Teachers--Training of--United States. 2. Teaching--United
States. 3. Education--Africa. I. Boudreaux, Gwendolyn M. Duhon.
II. Series.
LB1715.A72 1998
370'.71--DC21
                                   98-38871
                                       CIP

This is volume 38 in the continuing series
Mellen Studies in Education
Volume 38 ISBN 0-7734-8246-6
MSE Series ISBN 0-88946-935-0

A CIP catalog record for this book is available from the British Library.

The Edwin Mellen Press
Box 450
Lewiston, New York
USA 14092-0450

The Edwin Mellen Press
Box 67
Queenston, Ontario
CANADA L0S 1L0

The Edwin Mellen Press, Ltd.
Lampeter, Ceredigion, Wales
UNITED KINGDOM SA48 8LT

Printed in the United States of America

TABLE OF CONTENTS

2

Albany State University

Preface

Crafted by a cadre of experienced educators who prepare teachers for K-12 school systems throughout the country, this text is a compilation of insightful works that delineate strategies and techniques which speak to the changing landscape of education. This collection of chapters illustrates that today's educational institutions differ substantially from those of the past two decades.

With the demographic projection of a majority/minority rapidly becoming a reality, it seems safe to conclude that those who populate the K-12 schools, particularly the public schools, will be the groups that have been historically and systematically marginalized in this society. Relatedly, there is a body of statistics that suggest that those issues which have most affected and impacted the education of these groups --poverty, language barriers, and physical and emotional handicaps -- have been ignored in the system of American education.

This text not only alerts us to the fact that something in the educational system has gone awry, but it also provides a framework for addressing problematic issues and for improving preservice teacher training programs. These works suggest that the education of school children and the training of teachers must change from a standard, traditional mode to modes that are practical, empowering and more relevant to the experiences of the students.

The interdisciplinary nature of this volume gives it broad-based appeal. However, its primary audiences are those components of teacher education. Undergraduate students preparing for preservice teaching will find it useful. Through these discussions, students will come to understand that during their preservice experiences, they will be confronted with daily challenges. They will come to know that in addition to their being prepared with subject matter, they must be prepared for the multiplicity of events brought in each day by the variety of personalities of each class. They will begin to understand that originality, wit and physical and mental stamina must accompany their mastery of content if they are to become successful teachers.

It is likely that curriculum planners and theorists will find this volume helpful. They will come to acknowledge that curricula can not be limited to subject matter that is familiar to the masses. They will come to embrace the premise that curricula must lend to experimentation and innovation to promote discovery and inquiry, as well as to enhance creativity and independent thinking for correlating ideas, experiences and expressions. They will come to appreciate the notion that curricula must be sensitive to the lifestyles of the students.

Most unequivocally, the Colleges of Education in the nation's higher education system will find this volume valuable. These works underscore the need for flexibility in the colleges and universities so that they will continue to provide school children with motivated, well-prepared teachers.

Moreover, this text will make a significant contribution to the literature for the next century, for it is a volume of scholarship which brings a new dimension of professionalism to the field of teacher education.

Neari Francois Warner, Ph.D.
Acting Vice President for Academic Affairs
Grambling State University
Grambling, LA

Introduction

The face of education has changed drastically in the past twenty years. Shifts in demographics, socio-economic factors, and changes in majority/minority populations are requiring some teacher education programs to re-evaluate the way that preservice teachers are trained. The issues confronting educators and teacher education programs are more varied and complex than in years prior. Current educational practices must reflect the unique needs of the student population of the 1990's, as well as enhance the effectiveness of preservice teachers when working with diverse student populations. With the shift towards cross-curricular teaching, interdisciplinary approaches to preservice teacher training can be effective tools in improving the quality of education and preparation provided to preservice teachers.

This text on issues and practices in teacher education is an edited volume with submissions from numerous educators and academicians in teacher education. Twenty-four chapters are provided, some having multiple authors which will serve to provide differing viewpoints on the issues discussed and practices outlined. This text utilizes an interdisciplinary approach when addressing current issues and practices in teacher education. This text covers related topics in the areas of teacher training, early childhood education, professional ethics, post-baccalaureate certification, student empowerment, research, educational technology, cognition, aesthetic education, multicultural education, and others. A brief outline of those chapters are as follows:

Chapter 1 describes a method for establishing a knowledge base of active research procedures for pre service teachers through infusing sing research into a professional education course in student assessment. A case for enhancement of the teaching-learning process through research is also made.

Chapter 2 provides an operational definition for ethics and ethical behavior in both university classrooms and K- 12 settings. Additionally, a model for self-driven ethical decision-making that can be utilized for either preservice and inservice teachers will be provided.

Chapter 3 outlines the results of a study done on the reading readiness of a group of first grade learners. The purpose of this study was to determine the relative influence of preschool programs on the reading readiness of first grade children, given the level of home factors for support.

Chapter 4 addresses how African-American students perceive themselves and their role in this technological age. Suggestions will be included on how educators can address self-esteem issues in African-American students through the use of technology in the classroom.

Chapter 5 deals with the relationship between cognitive interactions of preservice teachers and the development of a strong knowledge base.

Chapter 6 focuses on how teachers can provide support to grieving children by creating a information-based support group that allows for expression of feelings in a safe, nurturing environment. Information on how to structure and conduct the group will be included.

Chapter 7 provides definitions for, distinctions between, and descriptions of existing post-baccalaureate teacher certification programs. Discussions about collaborations between post-baccalaureate teacher certification programs and traditional teacher certification programs will also be included.

Chapter 8 describes an empowerment project out of which came a model for student empowerment through the use of literature. The project goals, design, and outcomes will also be included.

Chapter 9 discusses empowerment as a tool for enhancing self-esteem, academic achievement, and the teaching/learning process. Strategies for empowering both teachers and students will be provided.

Chapter 10 provides suggestions and strategies for African-American adolescents in choosing appropriate peers for various kinds of relationships.

Chapter 11 provides a model/mechanism for first-year teachers to appropriately handle discipline problems and reinforce appropriate behaviors in their students.

Chapter 12 addresses specific issues and concerns related to higher education in West Africa and the resulting demands on West African educational systems. This chapter will also discuss the benefits of cooperation among institutions of higher learning in several territories in West Africa.

Chapter 13 outlines the challenges faced by the African educational system (both K- 12 and higher education) in meeting the academic and cultural needs of its' students and teachers.

Chapter 14 addresses the challenges and issues facing teacher education in Africa in the 21st century. A model for empowering teachers to face these problems with greater preparedness and certainty will be provided.

Chapter 15 discusses the findings of a study conducted to discover the frequency of primary school teachers' use of teaching aids in the course of teaching. The resulting effects of the use of those aids on pupils' academic performance will also be examined.

Chapter 16 examines the impact of guidance and counseling on students' academic achievement in school as well as the students abilities to adjust to ever-changing day-today social conditioning around them.

Chapter 17 focuses on one of the major communication problems in this society' as it relates to interaction, or the lack there of among students and the key adult figures in their lives.

Many adults are labeled "at-risk" without ever being an opportunity to find their'" places in society. Chapter 18 is centered around some of the problems which young adults, ages 18-22, face as they make futile attempts to enter into the world of work and take on responsibilities.

Chapter 19 presents content, activities/strategies, and materials which may be used in a teacher training program to demonstrate "how to" incorporate multicultural processes into the curriculum. Strategies, activities, and materials currently used to promote "Education That Is Multicultural" at Grambling State University will also be discussed.

Chapter 20 presents a sequential process for incorporating the CARE model into the K-12 curriculum. Emphasis will be placed on the rationale/need for utilizing such a model, as well as the utilization of the creative resources for developing positive self-concept, effective problem solving strategies, and other skills for promoting effective life-long decision-making skills.

Chapter 21 outlines and discusses basic components of a community enrichment program which is designed to develop and enhance cultural, academic, and life-long learning skills. This chapter will specifically include a description of activities and resources which are used during afterschool tutoring sessions and field-based experiences in the larger community.

Chapter 22 examines how instructional technology is used as a delivery system for students enrolled in the undergraduate teacher preparation programs and graduate programs in the College of Education at Albany State University in Albany, Georgia.

Chapter 23 outlines the results of a study of the implementation and effects of an interdisciplinary aesthetic education curriculum as an effort to increase the development of critical thinking. The effects are described during the initial

9

implementation years and ten years later. Emphasis is placed on forces which support and oppose critical thinking in school--forces within teachers and forces upon teachers in the schooling context and in the broader society.

Chapter 24 combines a theoretical overview of reading development with pragmatic teaching strategies to empower teachers for reading success.

This text would be invaluable to students, teachers, administrators, teacher educators, parents, and community members who are interesting in the appropriate and professional training of preservice teachers.

Gwendolyn Duhon-Boudreaux,

Editor

CHAPTER 1

COMBINING STANDARDS WITH CHANGING TEACHER NEEDS: INTRODUCING TEACHER RESEARCH STRATEGIES TO PRESERVICE TEACHERS

Kathryn Newman, Ph.D.
Associate Professor
Grambling State University
Grambling, LA

Faculty and administrators in teacher education programs are being required to reevaluate their philosophies and practices to meet the conditions imposed by both standards for accreditation as well as challenges in meeting the needs of children. Teachers are required to possess greater knowledge bases than those who were certified even a decade ago (Alley & Jung, 1995; Cuickshank & Metcalf, 1990; Darling-Hammond, 1996; Feiman-Nemser, 1990; Ladson-Billings, 1995; & Levine, 1996). Teacher education programs are trying to meet this demand by enhancing and even cramming more information and experiences into their programs leading to debates about the optimal matriculation time (Jones-Wilson, 1996; Stallings & Kowalski, 1990). This chapter is an attempt to demonstrate one way of establishing a knowledge base of active research procedures through infusing research into a required class in assessment. The result is a group of preservice teachers who have demonstrated the fundamentals of research--posing questions, operationalizing terms, collecting and analyzing data, and finally, either drawing conclusions or posing questions for future research.

Preservice teachers must have an exposure to both assessment and research. This exposure will help teachers construct a knowledge base of research as well as assessment practices along with limitations and advantages so that these teachers may be active participants in the both processes, not just consumers of data. The ideal teacher would then understand the process well enough to be an

11

effective liaison between the educational institution and the parents and community, as well as an advocate for best practice in assessment in order to secure the best assessment measures and evaluators for the student.

Additionally, preservice teachers should not only study current research, but also apply it to their future teaching. I believe that at this point the preservice teachers' knowledge bases break down. From a constructivist approach, learners (i.e., preservice teachers) must build their own understanding of the concepts in order to use them (Spivey, 1997). Unfortunately, research is usually presented in an abstract fashion such as citations in textbooks, or published articles that the student must secure and "analyze" or keep on file in idea banks. Rarely are the preservice teachers exposed to the process of research. Exposing teachers to the process would enhance their comprehension of the current knowledge base and increase their analytical skills. In fact, preservice teachers rarely are given the privilege of seeing research as a dynamic process. Consequently, I have observed that while many can read and summarize articles detailing current research, they have difficulty critically analyzing it for its usefulness, applying the research to themselves, or seeing themselves as vital parts of the research community (see also Holt-Reynolds, 1995). This is a serious problem for future educational change because as the demographics of students in the public schools change over the next 30 years, teachers will have to take a more active role in leading educational research to "best practices" and "best policies". To this end, we will have to have teachers in the field that can see more application of a particular research finding than a generic and mind-numbing "I think that' this is a very good article and I plan to use it in my teaching"

With these problems identified, I decided to insert a research component into a required preservice teachers' class in assessment. Students were already learning many of the terms and ideas about research that form the foundation including validity, reliability, assumptions of testing, and the mastery of basic statistics in order to further comprehend standardized test score reports. Vygotskian theory uses scaffolds to take a learner from one step to the next. It was decided that one of the next logical steps should be for the preservice teachers to complete an actual research study. Given the confines of the time, it was then decided to keep the research to a bare bones idea of generating a research question, identifying a population of interest, determining what behaviors would be examined, how those behaviors would be operationalized, creating a codesheet,

12

collecting the data, completing a simple analysis of the data, and drawing conclusions.

The research was grounded in an area that the preservice teachers had a great deal of practice with--watching their peers. The decision was made to confine the research population to peers in order to utilize the most familiar context to test the new skills. After introducing the students to the idea of doing behavioral research, and I had to alleviate the initial sense of "panic". Therefore, to demonstrate the applicability of research and observation techniques I asked the class where were good places to observe "behavior' or just to people watch. This generated a fertile ground of potential places to gather data. Next, we discussed how to operationalize the variables observed so that someone not with them could know exactly what they were observing and including in a more generic category such as "boredom". In fact, I found that the more outrageous the behavior, the easier it was to operationalize. They were then instructed that they could choose between observing at least five levels of one general behavior, or at least five unrelated behaviors that were grouped in a general theme such as "playing a video game". Ground rules for ethical research were established including: (1). use no real names to preserve confidentiality; (2). do not engage in research, no matter how intriguing, that they would not wish someone to complete on them; (3). the class itself was off-limits; (4). keep the language and tone neutral; and (5). report what was found, even if this was contrary to what they expected to find. These students had read the dubious history of intelligence testing, and it was felt that as new researchers, if they were trained correctly, they would not be as likely to make the mistakes of others.

The research training was simple. Students were given information and practice in using event recording and time sampling techniques. Cohorts in the class who had been trained secretly to use an example of each, then presented results of watching areas of the room for such behaviors as off-task and on-task (both had been operationalized beforehand). The process was reiterated during the next class period. This second period of instruction produced even more comprehension questions, demonstrating that there is more than one way to construct knowledge. We all need a foundation, but not all of us start laying it at the northwest corner.

Following the initial examples, students gathered at least 20 minutes of data. Their writeups of their research were short, but contained many of the same benchmarks of more traditional research. Specifically, their write-ups included the

13

actual codesheets that they constructed to collect their data, their codebooks which detailed how they operationalized their behaviors, and a one to two page synopsis of their research questions, what they did, what they found, and their interpretations of their research.

The results were intriguing. Social settings, worship services, study groups, and classes became research areas. As expected, a few did the minimum. Others employed creativity, humor and insight. Some tried the impossible, such as collecting data on a group of 50 students in a class, but Still came back with insights into classroom management and educational practice that seemed to be a reflection of what was found. In fact, of the sample of 25 research projects, eight tried to observe ten or more subjects at the same time. Eleven of the projects examined small groups of less than seven, and four of the projects looked at either single subjects or the behavior of a single couple. Two of the preservice teachers actually chose to observe in an elementary school, thus skipping the more familiar step to try their skills in their professional field.

Further analysis revealed spontaneous use of limiting strategies. Some observed first, then designed their codesheets in order to back and capture the behaviors being demonstrated ("After watching the boys play Mortal Kombat II for a while I came up with what I call the six types of video game players"). Others increased the amount of time that they observed in order to chart differences such as females vs. males, or early vs. late classes.

At the time they submitted there research projects, eighteen members of second class in assessment agreed to complete a short questionnaire concerning their feelings about the research. Of these 18, five reported no prior experience in research, nine reported that they had participated in one or two projects, and four reported participating in three or more research projects. When asked about their feelings upon hearing about the required research project, most of those without much experience expressed confusion, reluctance, and neutrality. Those with more experience tended to view it more positively. After the second class training session they reported feeling much more excited and confident My last question moved the preservice teachers from the now familiar to the slightly unfamiliar. When asked on a one to five scale (with five being "difficult") how easy would it be for them to create a second "study" to observe classroom behaviors in a school, the mean for the total group was 1.56 indicating that they felt more confidence.

This research training had another motive. As teachers in classrooms that would be more and more inclusive, they would have to be able to separate feelings

14

from facts in assessing students. The terms "hyperactivity", "slow", and "gifted" have been shown over time to be as much a reflection of teacher perception as of actual child behavior. Consequently, the effective and reflective teacher would need to be able to construct and objectively use some type of measure to determine if the difference is merely one of perception or of actual difference. One added bonus that I observed was the preservice students' new abilities to operationalize behaviors that they saw in schools. The preservice teachers needed to experience the fact that research is not static, nor confined to a laboratory, nor are they outside of the research arena. Through participation in the research activity they can perceive themselves to be a part of the research culture and invest more effort in the active analysis and evaluation of existing research, hopefully resulting in more direct involvement in research and policy making activities.

These results generate further questions. First, will the experience help to create teacher researchers? Second, will the experience aid the preservice ice teachers in their analyses of published research? Third, will the skills generalize to other situations in the classroom where the teacher might need to collect data (e.g., precision teaching, behavior interventions, portfolio creating)? Fourth, will it lessen some of the subjectivity in teaching? Fifth, will it strengthen the bonds between university- and field-based research?

References

Alley, R., & Jung, B. (1995). Preparing teachers for the 21st century. In M.J. O'Hair & S. Odell (Eds.), Educating teachers for leadership and cban2e (pp.285-301). Thousand Oaks, CA: Corwin Press, Inc.

Cruikshank, D.R., & Metcalf, K.K. (1990). Training within teacher preparation. In W.R. Houston (Ed), Handbook of research on teacher education (pp.469-497). New York: Macmillan Publishing Co.

Darling-Hammond, L. (1996). The quiet revolution: Rethinking teacher development. Educational leadership, 53(6), 4-10.

Feiman-Nemser, S. (1990). Teacher preparation: Structural and conceptual alternatives. In W.R. Houston (Ed), Handbook of research on teacher education (pp.212-233). New York: Macmillan Publishing Co.

Gay, L. R. (1996). Educational research 5th ed. Englewood Cliffs, NJ: Merrill.

Gould, S.J. (1981) The mismeasure of man. New York: W.W. Norton.

Holt-Reynolds, D. (1995). Preservice teachers and coursework: When is getting it right wrong? In M.J. O'Hair & S. Odell (Eds.), Educating teachers for leadership and change (pp.117-137). Thousand Oaks, CA: Corwin Press, Inc.

Jones-Wilson, F. (1996). Teacher standards: "Front-burner" news again. Dialogue, 6, 1-6.

Ladson-Billings, G. (1995). Multicultural teacher education: Research, practice and policy. In J.E. Banks & C.A. Banks (Eds.), Handbook of research on multicultural education (pp.747-762). New York: Macmillan Publishing.

Leedy, P.D. (1993). Practical research 5th ed. Upper Saddle River, NJ: Prentice Hall.

16

Levine, M. (1996). Educating teachers for restructured schools. In F.B. Murray (Ed). The teacher educator's handbook (pp. 620-647).San Francisco: Jossey-Bass.

Spivey, N.N. (1997). The constructivist metaphor. San Diego, CA: Academic Press.

Stallings, J.A., & Kowaiski, T. (1990). Research on professional development schools. In W.R. Houston (Ed), Handbook of research on teacher education (pp.251-263). New York: Macmillan Publishing Co.

Vygotsky, L. (1962). Thought and language. Cambridge, MA: The MIT Press.

CHAPTER 2

Professional Ethics in Education: Process and Practice

Gwendolyn Duhon-Boudreaux, Ph.D.
Assistant Professor
McNeese State University
Lake Charles, LA

Halloway C. Sells, Ph.D.
Professor
The Union Institute
Cincinnati, OH

When beginning a discussion about professional ethics in education, there are several terms which require operational definitions. Ethics can be defined as that branch of philosophy that deals with the rightness or wrongness of actions-deontological ethics-or with the goodness or badness of the motives and results of actions-axiological ethics (Young, 1995). It is also used to refer to a set of rules, principles, or a way of thinking that claims authority to guide the actions of a particular group. On other occasions it stands for the systematic study of reasoning about how we ought to act (Hira, 1996). Hira (1996) goes on to assert that

the moral imperative is not to do the right thing, but to be the right thing.

Ethics is about integrity, honesty. and compassion.

A working definition for professional ethics in education is the organized and systematic articulation of values related to educational practices and their application to the issues encountered in those practices. Professional ethics can also be thought of as representing the values of the field of education to which this field holds a common commitment. It's role is best seen as educative and consciousness raising. Ethics serves to raise the consciousness of the individual practitioner, the profession, and the larger community (Mattingly, 1995).

The process of assisting preservice teachers and educators with developing and adopting a code of professional ethics is not an easy undertaking. Many university teacher preparation programs do not offer specific courses on professional ethics or handling ethical dilemmas that can arise in schools or classroom settings. Many instructors rely on the curriculum, methods courses, and

19

student teaching experiences to provide preservice teachers with the necessary tools to effectively address ethical dilemmas that occur once they reach the classroom. Unfortunately, this approach does not take into consideration the individual differences in moral beliefs and attitudes that exist among preservice teachers as well as the faculties that serve them.

A review of the existing literature revealed several approaches that seek to create a mechanism for developing a professional code of ethics and addressing ethical dilemmas in education. Most involve generating a list of identifiaNe values related to the particular field of education, creating an environment where dialogue among professional can occur, and encouraging educators and prospective educators to consider their own personal beliefs, values, and morals when confronting ethical issues in their profession.

The National Association for the Education of Young Children (NAEYC) represents those working primarily with young children. NAEYC has produced the most advanced work in ethics in early childhood education through a large, partially externally funded project. This project, with the assistance of a consultant philosopher specializing in professional ethics, did the following in active exchange with association members:

a. Developed a working list of core professional values in an interactive discussion process at professional meetings;

b. Solicited and categorized ethical dilemmas of concern to practitioners;

c. Developed a process for the discussion of professional ethics

d. Circulated selected ethical dilemmas for discussion by the membership;

e. Developed differentiated ethical analyses of selected dilemmas;

f. Published a differentiated Code of Ethical Conduct and Statement of Commitment; and

g. Established an Ethics Panel to guide ethics work in the National association (Mattingly, 1995).

Young (1995) introduced the idea of logical levels of *good* as a means to help educators and preservice educators think their way through qualitative dilemmas. Level 1 identities the personal good of the teachers. Level 2 is the good of the students. Level 3 is the good of society. Level 4 represents the good of the earth community. Educators are frequently faced with situations in which they must choose between what they consider to be good, and what some other individual, agency. or constituency considers to be good. Young went on to assert that by better understanding these levels of good and the sources of the alternatives faced by educators and preservice educators, and by recasting their dilemmas in terms of the good each party is trying to achieve, educational professionals may have an easier time grappling with the ethical dilemmas thrust in their paths.

Thom Garfat and Frances Ricks has developed a self-driven ethical decision-making model that combines knowledge of the self, the profession's code of ethics, and problem solving techniques in helping child and youth care workers become competent in ethical decision making. This approach is centered in the self of the worker. In the context of clinical practice, the worker's personal framework, codes of ethics, and standards of practice are confronted, evaluated, and actualized through the self and applied to the situation and the process of problem-solving. The result of this activity is a self-driven ethical decision informed by the self, the situation, and the process of critical and reflective analysis in he current context. Following the decision, any action taken is evaluated to provide feedback to the problem-solving process as necessary and to the worker's framework (lens), which is validated or modified to respond to future situations (Garfat & Ricks, 1995).

Garfat and Ricks have identified several attributes necessary for self-driven practice:

1.   Knowing self;
2.   Thinking critically;
3.   Taking responsibility
4.   Considering alternative choices
5.   Evaluating and feedback (Garfat & Ricks, 1995).

This model for ethical decision making is not an easy one to embrace. It can be an uncomfortable and painful experience for a worker, educator, or preservice teacher to confront their own values, beliefs, and life-positions (Ricks, 1993). However, absolute reliance on external rules and guidelines is not only poor clinical practice. it is unethical practice. A self-driven approach such as this one allows for the respect of the uniqueness of each individual and the specific context (Garfat & Ricks, 1995).

Finally in assisting preservice teachers and educators with developing and adopting a code of professional ethics, teacher educators bear the responsibility of modeling professional, ethical behavior in their methods of instruction, classroom practices, and interactions with students and colleagues. Ethical dilemmas occur regularly in college classrooms and on university campuses. The professional and ethical treatment of these situations determines to a great extent how preservice teachers will address educational ethical dilemmas of their own.

References

Garfat, T. & Ricks, F. (1995). Self-driven ethical decision-making: A model for child and youth care. Child & Youth Care Forum,24(6), 379-391.

Hira, T. (1996). Ethics: personal and professional implications. Journal of Family and Consumer Sciences, 88(1), 6-9.

Mattingly, M. (1995). Developing professional ethics for child and youth care work: Assuming responsibility for the quality of care. Child & Youth Care Forum,24(6), 379-391.

Young, D. (1995). Understanding ethical dilemmas in education. Educational Horizons,24(1), 37-42.

Ricks, F. (1993). Therapeutic education: Personal growth experiences for child and youth care workers. Journal of Child and Youth Care, 8(3), 17-34

CHAPTER 3

THE IMPACT OF PRESCHOOL PROGRAMS AND HOME FACTORS ON THE READING READINESS OF FIRST GRADE LEARNERS

Tamara Lindsay Roberts, Ph.D.
Director of the Office of Professional Laboratory Experiences
Grambling State University
Grambling, LA

The purpose of this study was to determine the relative influence of preschool programs on the reading readiness of first grade children, given the level of home factors for support. The study attempted to determine whether preschool settings tended to be associated with readiness for reading, when home factors were held constant. The subjects were 120 first grade students enrolled in three public schools serving a middle and upper class population in a northwestern Mississippi city of 56,000 persons. All had attended preschool programs classified as structured, less structured, or unstructured. Data were obtained from questionnaires and release forms sent to parents. After permission was obtained, the reading readiness scores for the *Boehm Test of Basic Concepts* were recorded. A survey was designed and given to 16 preschool directors. The results of the study indicated that there were no significant differences found in the reading readiness scores of students who attended structured preschool programs from those who attended less structured programs, or from students who attended unstructured programs when the effects of home factors were eliminated. There was a significant relationship between the home and reading scores.

The current rate of illiteracy has come under close scrutiny with reference not only to the education of future citizens, but to the population at large. Horodesky (1981) states that despite humans' intellectual prowess and esteemed place in the hierarchy of the animal kingdom, their greatest challenges remain not in conquering space nor in perfecting technology, but in providing for the educational needs of their young. All types of values are undergoing changes, and it is not easy to pass on a cultural heritage as it once was.

According to Robinson (1970), few children are retained in school be-cause they have trouble with arithmetic, but if a child is "below grade level" in reading, particularly in the primary grades, he is considered failing. Therefore, children need to be literate in order to function effectively in schools and this society. As a result of the high failure rate in reading, educators began to look for ways to improve children's success. This effort to reduce school failure, and the public criticism of education mentioned earlier threw the spotlight on young children and on beginning reading.

The spotlight turned first to formal programs for young children and their potential for establishing skills and attitudes, prerequisites to the successful mastery of reading; and then to the home, the major sustaining environment for early learning. The home-related research has probably been more successful in establishing clear relationships between adult behavior and children's success as readers (Durkins, 1964; Brzeinski, 1964; Sheldon, 1952; Sutton, 1969; George, 1972; Dix, 1976). Moreover, as emphasis on the need for literacy increased, many preschool programs changed in focus. Parents demanded preschools and programs that would teach reading skills. Many parents felt that traditional play-oriented preschool and public school programs that emphasize socialization were not preparing their children for college or for earning a living. Prechool which stressed cognitive learning became popular with parents who wanted to give their children both an early start and a good foundation in learning.

Empirical research has not been conclusive as to the effect of preschool experiences on reading readiness. This study was designed to determine if a significant difference existed between the reading readiness scores of first grade students who attended structured, less structured, or unstructured preschool, while the home factors that influence reading preparations were held constant.

REVIEW OF RELATED LITERATURE

The contents of preschool programs have been carefully examined and their effectiveness evaluated. while sharing some common goals, early education programs differ widely in philosophies of child development, curriculum materials, teaching methods and learning environments. Preschool programs have been classified into broad categories. One grouping has been called child structured or academic mode; another is called child development or less structured; and another custodial or unstructured (Anselno, 1978). The discussion that follows gives an overview of preschool programs.

Structured Preschool Programs

Many educators have been concerned with the teaching of academic skills and the adjustment of a young child to formal schooling; however, there are many programs throughout the country that stress academic skills for preschool children. Bereiter and Engelmann's (1966) is representative of structured preschool programs. This program was a highly structured academic skill-oriented preschool program. Major objectives of the program were to develop the effective use of language concepts, to master certain arithmetic skills such as adding, subtracting, multiplying and counting; and to master and distinguish between verbal and visual symbols. Assumptions of the program are that the greatest needs of children are in the areas of language development and specific factural knowledge, and the basic concepts and specific learning skills in the program were selected to prepare children for successful academic performance in formal schooling.

Another highly structured academic-oriented program is the Weikart (1969) program in the Ypsilanti public schools; this program was known as "verbal bombardment." Cognitive lessons used in the academic curriculum were structured by placing emphasis on developing an intensive language environment, thinking skills, impulse control, and task orientation. The main objective of the program was to facilitate a positive change in the intellectual growth which would lead to academic success and social adjustment in the elementary grades.

Academic skills have been considered important for both disadvantaged and advantaged children. Fowler (1968) and Moore (1961) advocated early reading instruction for disadvantaged children. Both of these educators regarded effective programmed instruction as a means of enabling children to read and write before first grade. As a preparation for formal schooling, Widmer (1970) regarded the preschool years as a time for readiness activities which would be helpful in first grade.

Less Structured Preschools

27

A less structured traditional preschool based on the developmentalist learning theory can be described as a child-centered program. In such a program, language is seen as developing along with social and physical development. In this type of school, curricula are generally flexible, open, and often develop from the interest of the children. Teachers tend to explain a great deal to children, question them, and extend their language usage rather than model language for the child. Research points out that the development of the 'total child" is the focus of the less structured child development programs. Teaching strategies are low to moderate in structure. Children's needs are the basic factors in determining the activities such as building and developing vocabulary and experiences on trips. The Tucson Educational Model, the British Infant School Model, the Bank Street Model and the Educational Developmental Model are four examples of this type of program.

Unstructured Preschools

The third type of preschool pro-gram is the unstructured model. The atmosphere of many of these types of nursery, kindergarten, and preschool settings tends to approximate that of a home setting where learning is informal, unstructured, and unpressured. Talk and interactions with adults are spontaneous. The play and learning episodes are generally determined by the interest of the child and to some extent, that of the teacher; based on what she thinks is best for the children. In programs which pursue an in-formal approach to learning based upon play, the expected learning outcomes are socialization, emotional development, self-control, and tolerance for a setting which resembles a school. This group of behaviors is generally labeled pre-social behavior, indicating behavior which is necessary for getting along with one another and future school success (Morrison, 1980). To say that unstructured models do not educate is to ignore the fact that children always learn from their environment, regardless of its title. The question here is not whether or not this type model provides education. They all do. The important issue is the quality of the education. The unstructured model usually provides some preschool education activities during the day. There is abundant evidence that preschool programs have lasting effects on achievement and success in school. The teaching of reading in the preschool has been a major focus of attention for curriculum specialists and early childhood educators (Ballenger, 1983).

Attitudes toward reading and the way of life that reading creates are learned by children from both the conscious and the unconscious actions and feelings of the adults who surround them from their earliest years. This, of course, means especially, but not exclusively, their parents. This section describes evidences of the effect parents have on the cognitive growth and development of their children. Research has demonstrated that the home is the most important influence on a child's intellectual and emotional development. The growth and development of the preschool child reflects the home and environment in which he has been reared. Monroe (1951) believes it would be difficult to overstress the importance of the home environment because the cognitive and affective development of a child begins with his own parents, in his own home. The influence is irrefutable. Chomsky (1972) identified stages of early language development and observed that rapidity with which children grow through these stages is determined by the socioeconomic status and the reading interests of the children and their parents. Therefore, the quality of home and community experiences during the early years is crucial for children's future educational success. White (1975) concludes, "to begin to look at a child's educational development when he is two years of age is already much too late." Apparently. the first two years of children's lives may be particularly crucial in language learning. Bellugi (1971) contends that most language learning takes place well before children enter preschool. Anselno (1978) states that by preschool. children have mastered the most commonly used sentence forms. Although language development is a lifelong process, most of the basic learning has taken place by the time children enter school.

Parents who want their own children to be literate and well adjusted should be aware of, and involved in, facilitating pre-reading skills. Parents should be aware of the importance of their being models for their children, both through the quality of language in the home, and in reading books. Reading aloud to children as a means of introducing the child to print, introducing "book language," and offering the child more experiences seems to be a convincing enough argument for doing so. However, Flood (1977) did a study on the relationship between parental style of reading to young children and the child's performance on selected prereading related tasks. The research was conducted by taping parental

29

reading aloud sessions with the study group of 36 three-and-one-half to four-and-one-half-year old children in the San Francisco Bay area. Fourteen separate components of the parent-child reading episode were selected for analysis; and of these, four correlated significantly with the pre-reading scores. Stepwise regression techniques revealed the importance of six components of the parent-child reading episode. These steps were used to suggest a cyclical model involving four steps to produce positive results. Children profit from preparation for reading. Providing the child with a purpose for the reading activity is the first step. The second step is making children very much a part of the process; they need to talk about the story and relate it to their own experiences, and they need to be allowed to ask as well as answer questions about the book. The analysis of this study showed that adult-child verbal interaction can enhance the overall results of the reading session. The data also suggested that positive reinforcement from the parent is an effective component and makes up the third step. The final step is the evaluative questioning by parents. This step helps the child to clarify and learn to make conclusions and evaluations about the book read. For parent-child reading episodes to be successful, the parent should hold the child in his/her lap and read the stories over and over, thus making the child's first experiences with books good. In learning to read and in attaining favorable attitudes about academic endeavors, children are affected by both the stimulating experiences and the social-emotional climates in their home (Sartain, 1978).

The research discussed to this point seems adequately to support the importance of prereading experiences in the home. Ketcham (1966) used a questionnaire technique to study the background of 528 tenth grade students, and as a result, identified 26 family factors related to reading success at the .05 level of significance. The most important were:

1. The mother's use of the library;
2. The number of newspapers and good quality magazines in the home; and
3. The father's employment in professional, managerial, or technical work.

Other factors of special value were visits to museums and places of historical interest, discussions by parents of news and other items read, giving of books as gifts. and hearing classical music in the home.

According to Henderson (1981), rich and varied cultural experiences with interpretation are ideal. Play materials should facilitate Coordination of the

30

sensory-motor processes. Contact with adults who value achievement is essential; and an appropriate match between cumulative experiences and the children's current level of cognitive, social, and emotional organization is important (Henderson, 1981). The study by Woods (1974) has lent additional support to the theory that knowledgeable parents can enhance their children's prereading skills.

In order effectively to integrate the desired parental qualities mentioned in this section, parents need knowledge about how children develop. They need to know how to observe a young child. To help their children succeed, parents need informational and observational skills. Parents need to know how to take advantage of the setting, and common routines and activities in the home to create learning and problem solving opportunities for children (Honig, 1976). It is crucial that parents have a conscious awareness and acceptance of the teaching role they play in the lives of their children. Parents need to value the concept of providing experiences and environments conducive to producing competent children. Parents used in this study were of diverse backgrounds representing a cross section of socioeconomic status, even though schools were located in middle to upper middle class neighborhoods. The mean scores were based upon their response to questions relating to reading, oral expression and enrichment activities.

Methodology

The subjects for this study were 120 first grade students attending three public schools in northwest Mississippi. The population of this city is approximately 56,000. The school district that was in-involved in this research was selected because of its convenience, willingness to participate, and student population. The population of the school district's first grade classes at the time of this study was 830 children. The three schools from which subjects were selected were designated by the school officials as representing a cross section of socio-economic status from the first grade class. The schools listed their first grade enrollment combined as 300 students. All schools were located in middle to upper middle class neighborhoods. In the three schools where 300 first graders were identified, repeaters and non-preschool attenders were eliminated bringing the subject pool down to 232. Questionnaires were sent to parents of these subjects. Ninety questionnaires were returned; 56 parents did not wish to participate in the study; 10 students had attended preschools outside of the city; 45 questionnaires were never returned; and one student's preschool did not participate. As a result of

31

the personal telephoning, 30 more questionnaires were returned. A subject pool of 120 was left for consideration in the study.

The second group of data were the reading readiness scores from the *Boehm Test of Basic Concepts* obtained from the school records. The principal at each school gave the researcher a list which contained the children's names and reading raw scores. The third set were responses from preschool directors. Initially telephone calls were made to 22 directors to obtain permission for the researcher to visit. The school district chose the *Boehm Test of Basic Concepts Test* (BTBC) over other readiness tests on the basis of: (1) its clear, concise directions which, according to school officials, could easily be administered by aides or paraprofessional persons; (2) its reliability and (3) the fact that it could be administered to first grade children in small groups of eight to twelve. The parent survey questionnaire was designed by Drs. Mary M. Harris and Nancy Smith, Kansas State University. (Note 1). The instrument was developed by Smith from the literature review reported by Harris (1981). The test reliability as measured by Cronbach's coefficient alpha was 0.74. The data for this particular study confirmed Smith/Harris statistics by providing a coefficient alpha of 0.78.

A checklist was developed by the researcher for classification of the preschool centers into one of the three categories: (1) structured, (2) less structured, and (3) unstructured. The initial checklist was composed of 50 items. Items were to be rated by perceived importance to a preschool experience. The range of the scale was from 1 to 4, with the following equivalents: 1 = Very Important; 2 = Important; 3 Slightly Important; 4 = Not Important. The respondent was to circle the appropriate number. The Likert measurement scale was chosen because it represents a systematic and refined means for constructing indexes. In classifying a preschool, the researcher took the items categorized under the three types of schools and totaled them using the Likert Scale 1-4. Each of the three totals was then divided by the number of items in the group. When each preschool had three scores, the lowest was used to classify it.

TABLE I

Classification of Items On Preschool Director's Instrument

Structured Preschools:

1. Reading readiness is a very important part of the preschool program.
2. The preschooler will learn to print his/her name.
3. The preschooler will have good eye/hand coordination as exhibited by coloring within the lines.
4. The preschool program should prepare children for entry into first grade.
5. Academic learning should be a vital part of the preschool program.
6. The educational background of the preschool teacher is important.
7. Blocks of time in the preschool schedule should he designated for specific activities.
8. The preschooler will develop visual discrimination skills.
9. Preschool should provide the child with opportunities for verbal discussion and recognition of alphabet (out of sequence).
10. Preschool teachers should begin initial consonant sound teaching.
11. Preschoolers should practice printing the alphabet daily.

Less Structured Preschools:
1. Preschool program should be designed to meet children's individual needs.
2. The preschool will fit the child's developmental level.
3. Preschool will develop auditory discrimination skills in children.
4. The preschoolers will self-select activities some time during the day.
5. Preschoolers will develop skills in planning and solving problems.
6. Learning renters should he a very important part of the preschool program
7. The preschool will provide opportunities for the child to hear and express his perceptions of what he hears.
8. Preschool should provide the child with "discovery type' activities.
9. Preschool should provide opportunities for the child to verbalize his thinking processes as he/she is involved in a task.
10. Dictation of experience stories and recording of verbal experiences should be a part of the preschool program.
11. The preschool program emphasis is placed more on processes and experiences than on outcome.

Unstructured Preschools:
1. Children should he in preschool to allow parents and children "constructive time away from each other;
2. The preschool will provide sharing time (show 'n tell).

33

3. The educational background of the teacher is not as.. important as the love of children.

4   Preschoolers should develop a positive self-concept.

5. Preschoolers need plenty of time during the day to play.

6.   The preschooler will learn to control his/her emotions.

7. The preschool curriculum should be planned by the teacher as opposed to parents or a board of directors.

8. The preschool program should be flexible.

9. Preschool should promote completion of a task.

10. Exploration of movement with and without music should be a part of the preschool program.

11. The emphasis in preschool should be placed on socialization/emotional development.

The items in the preschool instrument were subjected to the Cronbach Test of Reliability to determine if the items were internally consistent. The alpha coefficients revealed a reliability of .95 on the structured items, .88 on the less structured items, and .86 on the unstructured items. The analysis of covariance was used to determine what proportion of the dependent variable, preschool type. is nonmetric or categorical while the covariate, home reading background is metric. Prior to the use of ANACOVA procedures, regression procedures were employed to test for interaction effects. The Pearson Product Moment Correlation was also calculated to determine the relationship between home factors and the preschool. For these statistical techniques, the .05 confidence level of significance was selected to evaluate if differences existed between the three independent groups.

Table II presents a description of how the preschool programs in this study were classified into one of the three groups identified by the scale. The lowest number of the three scores in Table II indicated the group into which each preschool was classified. Schools 1, 11, 12, and 16 were Head Start Centers. Of the three centers one was church-related. Three of the directors felt their schools were structured; one saw her program as both structured and less structured. On the basis of the checklist, this school was actually classified as unstructured. Two of the other schools, 11 and 12, were classified as less structured, although one of them, school 12, scored almost equally low on the structured scale. School 1 was classified as structured.

Schools 13, 5, and 8 were public school Chapter 1 programs. Each director saw these programs as structured in nature because the goal of the programs was to prepare children for entry into first grade. Further checking showed that school 5 rigorously followed a structured reading curriculum, while schools 8 and 13 provided more free choice time. The three directors of semiprivate schools, 6, 7, and 14, saw their programs as less structured and structured. Two of the three church-related preschool directors, 9 and 15, saw their missions as unstructured. These preschools were the child's home away from home and the mother image was being projected. One of the church school directors (4) felt she should follow the academic approach with emphasis on involving the home as much as possible. However, most of the preschools only involved the parents through print (i.e., newsletters, notes and progress reports).

TABLE 11

Classification Of Preschool Programs

I.D. No.	Structured	Less Structured	Unstructured	Classification	
1	1.36	1.54	1.72	Head Start	S
2	1.18	2.09	1.90	Private	S
3	1.72	2.00	2.36	Montessori	S
4	1.90	2.18	2.18	Church	S
5	1.90	2.00	2.27	Chapter 1	S
6	1.27	1.09	1.36	Semi-Private	L
7	3.72	2.81	2.90	Semi-Private	L
8	1.90	1.36	1.45	Chapter 1	L
9	1.54	1.45	2.00	Church	L
10	3.72	2.81	2.90	Private	L
11	2.81	2.36	2.45	Head Start	L
12	2.09	2.00	2.36	Head Start	L
13	1.75	1.45	1.34	Chapter 1	U
14	3.63	2.54	2.36	Semi-Private	U
15	3.36	2.54	2.36	Church	U
16	3.54	3.45	2.36	Head Start	U

Total Preschool Programs = 16

35

The director of school 10, an upper class private center, felt her total program was academic. Children were required to wear uniforms and sit at desks, as in formal school. The tuition was very expensive, mostly children of professional parents were in attendance. School 3 considered itself a Montessori school, although it was not licensed by Montessori Association. However, it adhered to the Montessori principle of the prepared environment. One of the patterns that emerged here was that 14 directors said their programs were structured, but this did not prove to be so for nine of these programs when rated by the scale devised for the study. Why this is so provides an interesting starting point for speculation. Table III shows a breakdown of the 120 subjects, by attendance, at the structured preschools, less structured preschools, and unstructured preschools used in this study.

Evaluation Of Stated Hypothesis

Two null hypotheses were formulated for the study. The two null hypotheses are listed and statistical findings are evaluated in terms of each hypothesis. Hypothesis 1: When home scores are utilized as covariate, there will be no significant differences between the reading readiness scores of students who attended structured preschool, less structured, or unstructured preschools.

TABLE III

Number of Children By Preschool Type

Structured		Less Structures		Unstructured	
School	N	School	N	School	N
1	5	6	11	13	5
2	7	7	6	14	5
3	5	8	7	15	4
4	6	9	6	16	5
5	11	10	4		
		11	26		
				12	7
	34		67		19

Total N - 120

36

Findings: Least-squares analysis of covariance applied to mean scores of the three preschool groups produced an F value of .404, which is not significant at the .05 level. Decision: Based on the findings, the first null hypothesis was retained. Hypothesis 2: There is no significant relationship between the home factor and reading readiness scores. Findings: Analysis of variance produced a significant covariate with an F value of 6.231. Decision: Based on the findings, the second null hypothesis was rejected. Looking at reading scores by school types with parent score as covariate determined whether there was a significant covariate (see Table IV). On the reading tests scores for the *Boehm Test of Basic Concepts,* no significant differences between the unadjusted means were found at the .05 level of significance. The F value of 6.231 was considerably above .05. Therefore, there were no significant differences between the three preschool groups. When parent ratings were accounted for; the mean score on the readiness test changed. Table V shows that the structured school means changed to 39.22; less structured changed to 38.24: and unstructured changed to 37.07.

Summary Of The Results

1.   There was no significant difference found in the reading readiness scores of students who attended structured preschool programs, those who attended less structured programs, or students who attended unstructured programs when the effect of home factors was eliminated.

2.   There was a significant relationship between the home and reading scores.

TABLE IV

Analysis Of Variance Reading Scores By

School Type With Parent Score As Covariate

Source of Variation	Degrees of Freedom	Sums of Squares	Mean Scores	F-Ratio
Home Score (Covariate)	1	387.551	387.551	6.231*

Between Groups (Preschools)	2	50.284	25.142	.404
Within Groups (Preschools)	116	7214.462	62.193	
Total	119	7652.262	64.305	

Significant at .05 level.

Discussion/Conclusions

Based on the findings in this study, it was concluded that the type of preschool a child attends does not impact his/her reading readiness scores once the effect of home factors are removed. It would appear that the home has a significant impact on reading readiness scores. The relationship of the home factors with the readiness scores of preschool children was studied. This relationship was significant, which gives indication that higher parent scores tend to be associated with higher readiness scores. Parents who scored high on the survey seem to have children who scored high on reading readiness test. The findings of this study revealed that most parents placed a great importance on early learning. From the review of related literature, Monroe (1951) believes it would be difficult to over-stress the importance of the home environment because the cognitive and affective development of a child begins with his own parents, in his own home. The influence is irrefutable. The findings of this study have verified a strong point in the literature that home experiences make an impact on students' achievements. This is especially true for home experiences in reading as related to the reading readiness scores.

TABLE V

Readiness Scores By School Type

Means	Unadjusted	Adjusted For Home Scores
Structured	39.51	39.22

38

| Less Structured | 38.12 | 38.24 |
| Unstructured | 37.06 | 37.07 |

The parent scores were randomly distributed among preschool programs; therefore, parents who scored high on home survey did not necessarily send their child to a certain type of preschool program. The findings of this study revealed that preschool directors placed importance on being labeled 'structured." The belief of a person that a school is structured is not necessarily so; maybe being structured is fashionable right now in light of early reading. Structured preschools seem to be the trend. In spite of the desire for being labeled structured, preschools of several types are identified. The type of preschool did not appear to affect reading readiness scores. Based on the data of this study, it would seem clear that the state of Mississippi, when evaluating its new state-wide preschool programs, would be wise to direct programs to develop an eclectic approach rather than using one specific methodology or structure. These programs should also cultivate family involvement in children's learning no matter what type program is being adopted. Although a casual relationship cannot be inferred from the data presented here, it appears that the type of preschool program a child attends is not nearly as important as the quality of education received from the program.

In order to insure quality education, administrators in Mississippi should make certain that the mandated kindergarten programs are related to the total programs that already exist in the school system. They should see that teachers provide proper curriculum balance that includes reading for those students who are able. Additional preparation for those teachers who require it should also be provided. The administration should be careful to hire and/or encourage kindergarten teachers who have a basic foundation in reading and language development. All primary teachers should be exposed to the preschool curriculum, thus assuring continuity within the department. If tenured teachers have little or no background in early childhood education, they should be encouraged to upgrade their preparation by taking reading and language arts method courses designed especially for teachers of young children. Teachers and aides should also be encouraged to attend in-service workshops that will improve their skills.

Accreditation standards for public schools and for teacher education programs should include requirements for specific preparation in appropriate reading methodology and in parental involvement. In developing accreditation standards, administrators, teachers, and parents should be directed to the joint

39

statements of the National Association for the Education of Young Children (NAEYC), the Association for Childhood Education International (ACEI), International Reading Association (IRA), Association of Supervision and Curriculum Development (ASCD), the National Council of Teacher Education (NCTE), and the National Black Child Development Institute (NBCDI), for concerns about present practices and recommendations from these professional organizations. It is recommended that further studies and experiences in preschool education or early childhood education programs be required for certification and recertification of early childhood educators and made available to parents. The approaches covered should include parent education and training to improve child rearing practices and attitudes; a wide range of health, recreation, and educational services; and the use of mass media.

Parents from all socioeconomic backgrounds need and should be involved in the decision making process of the kindergarten programs. A wide range of options must be actually accessible to them. Procedures might run the gamut from intensive and systematic training to the general improvement of the environmental setting in which children and their parents live. A variety of activities are available to school systems to promote parental involvement, such as teaching mothers how to improve children's language skills, for example. Other parent groups have focused on increasing parental self-awareness, knowledge of ways to motivate children, home management skills, or making and learning materials. This type of parental involvement could also entail the parent-toy-lending library. At the once-a-week parent meetings, new toys are introduced. The toy as a means to boost children's problem-solving skills is demonstrated, discussed, and illustrated in films. Books can also be introduced in this same way.

Parents can also be involved in early childhood education through: newsletters, parent bulletin boards, parent conferences, home visits, parent workshops, and volunteering regularly as teacher aides. These activities can serve to enhance parents' understanding of the school system, thus promoting greater understanding of both teacher and parents as they work toward a common goal. It is common in research of this type to recommend further study with such modifications as increased sample sizes or additional performance criteria. Such recommendations seem justified, as the data base examined was relatively small. Additional research in this area would most profitably be directed examining the classrooms of structured preschools, less structured preschools, and unstructured preschools for verification of hypotheses tested.

References

Anselmo, S. (1978). Improving home and preschool influences in early language development. The Reading Teacher, 11, 139-143.

Ballenger, M. (1983). Reading in the kindergarten. Childhood Education, (1), 186-187.

Bellugi, U. (1971). Simplification in children's language. In R. Huxley & E. Ingrams (Eds.), Language acquisition: Models and methods. New York: Academic Press.

Bereiter, C., & Englmann. (1966). Teaching disadvantaged children in the preschool. Englewood, NJ: Prentice-Hall.

Brzeinski, J. E. (1964). Beginning reading in Denver. The Reading Teacher, 18, 16-21.

Chomsky, C. (1972). Stages in language development and reading exposure. Harvard Educational Review, 42(1), 1-33.

Cohen, D. (1977). Kindergarten and early schooling. Englewood, NJ: Prentice-   Hall.

Dix, M. (1976). Are reading habits of parents related to the reading performance of their children? (ERIC Document Reproduction Service No. ED 133 693).

Flood, J. E. (1997). Parental styles in reading episodes with young children. The Reading Teacher, (5), 865-867.

Henderson, R. W. (1981). Parent-child interaction, theory, research, and prospects. New York: Academic Press.

Honig, A. S. (1976). Parent involvement in early childhood education. Washington, DC: National Association for the Education of Young Children.

Horodesky, B. (1981). Family forces for preschool development of health, vocabulary, and perceptual skills. Mobilizing family forces for worldwide reading skills. Newark, DE: International Reading Association.

41

Ketcham, C. A. (1966). The home background and reader self-concept which relate to reading achievement. Dissertation Abstracts, 28, 2-A, 499. (ERIC Document Reproduction Service No. P 420 004 485).

Monroe, M. (1951). Growing into reading: How readiness for reading develops at home and at school. New York: Scott Foresman and Company.

Nelson, K. (1973). Structure and strategy in learning to talk. Monographs of the Society for Research in Child Development, 38(1-2, Serial No. 149).

Robinson, H. (1970). Significant unsolved problems in reading. Journal of Reading, (11), 77-82.

Sartain, H. W. (1983). Research summary: Family contribution to reading attainment mobilizing family forces. Newark, DE: International Reading Association.

Sheldon, W. D., & Carrillo, L. W. (1952). Relation of parents, home, and certain developments to children's reading ability. Elementary School Journal, 1, 262-270.

Weikart, D. P. (1968). Ypsilanti preschool curriculum demonstration project. (ERIC Document Reproduction Service No. ED 046 503).

White, B. L. (1975). To begin to look at a child's educational development when he is two years of age is already too late. The first three years of life. Englewood, NJ: Prentice-Hall.

Widmer, E. L. (1970). The critical years: Early childhood education at the crossroads. Scranton, PA: International Textbook.

Woods, C. (1974). The effect of the parent involvement program in reading readiness scores. Mesa, AR: Mesa Public Schools. (ERIC Reproduction Service No. ED 104 527).

CHAPTER 4

TECHNOLOGY AND IMAGERY: A POSSIBLE SOLUTION

Brian 0. Williamson, M.Ed.
Department of Teacher Education
College of Education
Grambling State University
Grambling, LA

As the United States becomes more and more a nation inhabited by people of color, scholars are devoting more time to understanding different learning styles, cultural beliefs, and the devastating effect of low self-esteem. In recent years, traditional schools in the United States have come under careful scrutiny regarding its ability to adequately educate and prepare African-American students to compete in a global society. Carter Woodson (1933), in The miseducation of the Negro, stated that "unless African-Americans receive an education befitting to their peculiar situation, they will never fully enter into the economic, political and social institutions in the United States of America". Shade (1982) and Cohen (1969) support Woodson's statement by stating that the learning style of the African American is one that emphasizes field sensitive abilities as well as preference for person-oriented classroom activities and cooperative learning that focuses on people and what they do. With these statements in mind and the lack of positive Black representations within the African-American household, on television, textbooks and in other forms of media, it has become imperative for the school system to include a structure that will compensate for the different learning style and the absence of positive images within the school day.

As studies progress, researchers are finding that the development of mentor programs, after school programs, and the exposure to culturally correct textbooks and courses for African-American children are becoming important to their educational process, achievement, and self esteem. Moreover, the evidence is alluding to the statement that exposure to positive African-American role models and positive African-American imagery is the most powerful and influential force in these children's lives and the most significant deterrent of the social and individual problems of the young Black children.

Although African-American role models have been increasingly linked to the betterment of young African-American children both educationally and socially, the absence of positive Black imagery in the media and the school system has become an increasingly great problem. Tiedt and Tiedt (1995) state that students need to see realistic yet positive images of the lives of people like themselves. This absence has caused a self esteem and self love deprivation that usually results in deviant behavior, teenage pregnancy, high unemployment rates, and infrequent experiences of success in the academic arena.

Although a high self concept and the evidence of self worth and self love is greatly needed for academic and personal success, America has not made a whole scale effort to assure that these elements are in place for the African-American learner. Positive African-American images have not been depicted on a whole scale in the textbooks while the media has been used as a vehicle for "Black-Bashing". The media too often illustrates African-Americans as drug dealers, welfare mothers, deviants, or as only having significance in America due to the white person they are dating or associated with. This effort by the media to distort the significance and worth of African-Americans has elevated them to become America's least expected and least likely to succeed both academically and personally.

Positive African-American images both in the media and in the school system may be the needed factor to improve the academic performance of African-American students. By the time African-American students, especially African-American males, enter the fourth grade, many of them have already internalized the traditional school system's program for their failure and have begun to exhibit signs of intellectual regression as a result (Kunjufu, 1985 cited in Gill, 1991). Furthermore, researchers have pointed out the various discriminatory practices in America's public school system which include the absence of positive African-American images and people from the text books and curriculum. These practices and absences have been linked to the high minority student suspensions and placements in mentally or emotionally retarded classes (Cardenas and First, 1983 cited in Calabrese, 1990).

The plight of African-American students influenced by negative experiences and negative or lack of positive African-American images in the school system, has been more evident in African-American males and has partially contributed to their label of "endangered species". Statistics to support this phenomenon are overwhelming: Approximately 18% of African-American

44

males drop out of high school and African-American males are more than twice as likely to be unemployed than his white counterpart (Wright 1991, 1992), African-American males, while only comprising 6% of the total US population, represent 49% of the prison population, comprise 37% of school suspensions and 41% of all children in special education, 70% of African-American households are headed by single parents and only 4% of African-American males attend college (U.S. Census Bureau, 1990 cited in Gill, 1991).

It is also evident that the technological revolution is here to stay. America, with it's digital television and information super highway, is quickly becoming a country of cyber-cafes and cyber-schools. This paradigm shift to an electronic society, has brought with it the baggage of non-existent positive African-American images and nomenclature. Michael Marriot (1995) has found that the Internet is not marketed for the African-American. He supports his findings by stating that there is an absence of African-American use of the Internet in the commercials shown on television and that the whole genre of using the Internet, via the nomenclature of "surfing the web", has left the African-American out of the mix (Marriot 1995).

The information presented here is extremely significant in that it attempts to support the idea that exposing African-American learners to positive African-American images in the classroom via various forms of technology will increase the interest and success in their academic endeavors. Positive African-American images in a young African-Americans' life is hoped to increase their self-confidence and decrease their chance for failure in the school system and society as a whole. There is evidence that supports the theory that exposure to positive African-American images via technology will have an effect on the academic success of African-American students. Many educators and parents are seeking resolutions to the current state of black children. There have been many solutions proposed by clergymen, businessmen, educators and parents. No viable solution has been initiated yet.

The issues of a positive self image of a learner and the significance of the integration of technology into the curriculum have resulted in many differing opinions. Research has shown that African-American students who do not have exposure to positive African-American images have a low self concept of themselves. Educators are eager to find a solution to this devastating problem that plagues African-American students in the school system.

45

INTEGRATING TECHNOLOGY

The literature in this area has consistently shown the need to integrate technology into the school wide curriculum and that positive Black images must be depicted within the school day. Barbara Means, Kerry Olson and Ram Singh (1995) reported that technology must be tied to a coherent, school wide instructional agenda in order for technology to be effective in a school. Means, et. al. (1995), later stated that technology can provide students with access to a wide array of information, that schools should use a school wide approach, and that schools should use technology in the core curricula for all students.

Analysis of these statements suggest that technology is an essential element in the educational process of all students in the United States. The authors imply that technology should be used not just in a computer class, but should be used in all classrooms and in all courses of study. With technology providing access to infinite amounts of information, the integration of this medium into the classroom will provide the student with the opportunity to gather a plethora of diversified viewpoints and images that will assist in the self concept, self love, self image and self esteem building of the African-American student. These assumptions have been supported by Zane Berge (1993) when he stated that technology in the classroom will promote the "knowing of what" and the "knowing of why" as opposed to the traditional "knowing of what you see" and the "knowing of what you have been told". This, it is assumed, will lend itself to the notion that technology will give the African-American student the power to combat the negative or lack of positive images they see depicted in the various forms of media. Technology in the classroom will allow the student, as Berge (1993) later states, to find relationships between existing theories and phenomena that they may have read or have been taught. This will allow the African-American student to search for themselves to prove or disprove the negative images that have been forced upon them. Both Means, et. al.(1995), and Berge (1993) believe that technology should be used as a communication resource that can create student directed, theoretical learning projects, and connect the student to a network of people and information. Technology gives the African-American student the ability to fill the void of negativeness by connecting them with positive African-Americans from all over the world. This will also

46

allow the African-American student the have an "on-line mentor" or "cyber role model" that can support and guide the student through difficult times. The "on-line mentor" or "cyber role model" will be able to, via e-mail, answer questions pertaining to college, job opportunities or life. Using technology in this way, the African-American learner will no longer have to wait for the "designated" time to meet and speak with their mentors. They will be able to have access to their on-line mentor" or "cyber role model" any time they feel it is necessary to speak with them.

Integrating technology into the curriculum is demonstrated by Karin Wiburg (1994) exquisitely when she discusses how technology can be integrated into a science curriculum. Wiburg (1994) states that Telecomputing and Hypermedia will allow the student to *do* science rather than just read about it by giving the student the opportunity to participate in real science activities around the world. Wiburg (1994) later states that using Telecomputing will allow the students to have hands-on, project-oriented activities that will require student cooperation, problem solving, data collection, data analysis, investigations into real world problems, collaboration among other students in other parts of the country, and the direct contact with scientists from all over the world. Wiburg (1994) states that by using Telecomputing in the science classes has generated not only an enthusiasm in the learning process but also a genuine interest in science in general by those students who have previously demonstrated a lack of there of.

While Wiburg suggests the use of a computer, Poirot, et. al (1994) suggests that ordinary technologies, such as the telephone, handheld calculator and VCR, can be effective tools with assisting the educational process of at-risk students in the following ways: I) *Telephone* - It can be used as a mode of communication between teacher and parent either as a messaging center telling parents of pertinent information about their child or as a telecommunication devise so that the parent can, by using a home computer, link into a school encyclopedia or other homework aid. 2) Instructional Video - The school can send home videos for the family to view on such topics as study habits. 3) Handheld calculators/Instructional software - These aids can be used to supplement and assist the parent in helping their child. 4) Electronic grade books/progress reports - The teacher will be able to send home computer generated reports to the parents. These examples can be applied to the African-American learner. This implies that technology, no mater how small or ordinary, can make a difference in the education of a student.

47

IMAGES AND MULTICULTURAL EDUCATION

Research finds that the academic and intellectual self-esteem of African-American children, especially African-American males, declines with age (Wiener et al., 1993). Studies show that mentor programs, and the such, that put young African-American children with positive African-Americans have significant influence on the academic achievement of these children. Educators, along with many within the black community, believe that the African-American child is deprived of positive role models, positive images of African-Americans, and that this deprivation is at the root of the lack of self concept, self esteem, self image, and self love within the African-American.

It has been proposed that a multicultural or culturally pluralistic curriculum would eliminate this problem. Branch, et. al (1993) defines cultural pluralism as the relative absence of assimilation and the condition in which cultural groups are able to maintain their collective identities and membership in a single macro society. Branch, et. al. (1993) also state that many social organizations, such as the Anti-Defamation league of B'nai B'rith, advocate the use of culturally pluralistic materials during instruction.

These statements, along with Gill (1991) referencing the Egyptians belief that self knowledge was the basis of true knowledge and defining self image as the core of the self concept and a conscious appraisal of what one thinks he is, encompasses the notion that a positive African-American imagery will assist the African-American student to overcome the systematic image destroying perpetrated by the American school system. Many reports have stressed the need for students to feel good about learning and about themselves as learners. Biggs (1992), citing Pollard, states that social attitudes and self perceptions of ability are essential elements that will assist literacy instruction for African-Americans. Biggs (1992) later suggests that the use of anecdotes that reflect a positive African-American presence in society and the use of literature written by and pertaining to African-Americans are also essential to the African-American learner. These essential elements, however, have been conveniently left out of the instructional process for the African-American child. The African-American learner is inundated with negative words, like black-balled, pictures, historical facts, and literature written by and pertaining to the dominant culture throughout their school career. This inundation is further supplemented after the school bell rings via the television, album covers, album lyrics, magazines, newspapers, movies and the evening news. Every second, of every hour, of everyday, the African-American sees and hears only negatives things about himself. With the dominant culture forcibly fed to the African-American learner and the constant bombardment of negative images, it is no wonder that the African-American learner has had so much difficulty in society. This statement is reinforced by Hill (1985) when he stated that any group which fails to consciously and systematically frame the parameters in which the self image is processed, elevates the vulnerability of their young, promotes discontinuity and worse, sets the stage for potential group demise.

FACTORS THAT CONSTIPATE THE INTEGRATION

History dictates that change is a slow process. The educational system, unfortunately, is not immune to this fact. Dunn (1996) states that the slow rate of changing to a technologically based educational system could be due to the lack of administrative support, inadequate staff development, low quantity, quality and access of technology in the classroom, failure to allocate a technology coordinator, nonexistence of cursory plans for adopting and implementing technology into a school, lack of funds and personnel to maintain equipment, continual assessment of content acquisition through traditional methods, and establishment of a broad participatory clientele to establish a technology culture. Dunn (1996) later states that the lack of administrative support, due to the age of the administrator, is directly proportional to this rate of change. This suggests that one of the factors for the delay of the integration of technology could be unfamiliarity with technology by those in decision making positions. This assumption is suggested by Strommen (1993) in his evaluation of speech recognition software. Strommen's evaluation showed that this software was not effective with children. This demonstrates that this system, although creative and used within a school district, does not serve a purpose in a school.

Mcadoo (1994) states that the educational system is not experiencing a delayed reaction to technology, but rather, the educational system is experiencing a inequity in the use of the technology. She states that poorer schools, minority schools, and rural schools are using their technology as a remediation tool as opposed to the project oriented approach used in the rich, Caucasian schools.

Mcadoo (1994) supports her statements by citing a program in the state of Kentucky. She states that this program was designed to give the rural schools of Kentucky computers to compete in this digital society. This program, although noble, has given the rural schools of Kentucky a bunch of computers with the capacity to only do remedial work. This "effort" implies that learners not of the dominant culture, like the African-American learner, will always be the recipient of sub-standard technology. This assumption is supported by Kozol (1991) when he documented the inequity of technology and basic equipment of various districts throughout the country.

Another factor in the delay of the integration of technology is the teachers themselves. Hannafin, et. al (1993) state that over 60% of the teachers surveyed in 1989 did not use computers. This figure suggests that the teachers, like the previously mentioned administrators, are also computer illiterate. This illiteracy could be associated to the isolation of the teacher. Hoy and Tarter (1995), citing Girling, confirms this thought by stating that the organization of the schools are centered around self-contained classrooms which promotes a climate of professional isolation, hence limiting the opportunity to work collaboratively with experienced colleagues. This statement can be applied to technology. The isolation of the teacher, does not lend itself to that teacher learning of technology and its many uses from another teacher. Hannafin et. al, (1993) later state that most "breakthroughs" in education usually resulted in disappointment followed by disillusionment and eventually abandonment. This phenomena has created what Hannafin et al, (1993), citing Cuban (1986), denotes as the exhilaration-scientific credibility-disappointment-blame cycle. This disappointment, it is implied, has created a sense of apathy among the teachers which has caused the teachers to be very cautious when asked to implement something new.

Hannafin et al, (1993) also cite the following factors as a possible cause for the teacher's apathy towards technology: 1) Poorly designed software applications and lack of time to design their own software (Reiser and Dick, 1990); 2) The belief that computers do not improve the learning outcomes (Wiske et al. 1990); 3) The resentment of computers due to the perceived competition for the students' attention (McMahon 1990); 4) The risk of bucking an nonsuportive administrator, while other teachers identify the increased investment in time and effort (Cuban 1989); 5) The fear of losing "center stage" (Wiske et al 1990); 6) The need for a paradigm shift from teacher to facilitator (Hannafin 1993). These many citations establish the fact that the teacher has a fear of the unknown and that the embracing of technology will shift the authority from the teacher to the student. This shift puts the teacher in the uncomfortable position of not being the disseminator of information which could make the student the most knowledgeable person in the room.

CONCLUSION

The review of related literature has confirmed the need for schools and school districts to implement the inclusion of positive African-American images into the everyday curriculum. Most of the literature in this chapter has attributed the poor academic performance of African-American students to their low self concept, low self image, low self esteem, and the low self love. In addition, the literature review has illuminated the importance of technology in the classroom. Authors and researchers have postulated that the integration of technology into the curriculum makes a difference not only in what is learned but how the information is processed.

This review investigated the importance of technology to the curriculum. The authors cited stated how technology can give the learner access to unlimited information and will put the learner in charge of what is learned and when it will be learned. The authors also concurred that technology will give the learner access to other learners and scholared individuals throughout the world.

This review also concentrated on the negative images of African-Americans. The authors cited stated the significance of the self image to a learner. Finally, this review concentrated on the factors that are deterring the integration of technology into the school system. Both the administrator and the teacher have been cited by the authors as one of the deterring factors as was the lack of knowledge and isolation of the educational system.

References

Berge, Z. L. (1993). Beyond computers as tools: Reengineering education. Computers in the Schools 9, 167-177.

Biggs, S. A. (1992). Building on strengths: closing the literacy gap for African-Americans. Journal of Reading, 35, 624-628.

Branch, R., Goodwin, Y., & Gualteri, J. (1993). Making classroom instruction culturally pluralistic. The Educational Forum, 58, 57-70.

Gill, W. (1991). Issues in African-American education. Nashville, TN: One Horn Press

Hannafin, R., & Savenye, W. (1993). Technology in the classroom: The teacher's new role and resistance to it. Educational Technology 33, 26-31

Hare, N. (1985). Bringing the black boy to manhood. San Francisco: Black Think Tank.

Kozol, J. (1991). Savage Inequalities. New York: Crown Publishers.

Mcadoo, M. (1994, March). Equity: has technology bridged the gap? Electronic Learner, 24-34.

Marriott, Michael. (1995). Cybersoul not found. Newsweek, 35, 62-64.

Means, B., Olson, K., & Sign, R. (1995, September). Beyond the classroom restructuring schools with technology. Phi Delta Kappan, 69-72.

Poirot, J., & Robinson, G. (1994, March). Parent involvement and technology with at-risk students. The Computing Teacher, 44-45.

Ritchie, D. (1996). The administrative role in the integration of technology. NASSP Bulletin, 21-28.

Strommen, E. F., & Frome, F. S. (1993). Talking back to big bird: preschool users and a simple speech recognition system. Educational Technology Research and Development 41, 5-15.

Wiburg, Karin. (1994, April). Teaching science with technology: telecommunications and multimedia. The Computing teacher, 6-8.

Woodson, C. (1933). <u>The mis-education of the Negro</u>. New York: AMS Press.

CHAPTER 5

INCREASING LEVELS OF COGNITIVE INTERACTIONS IN PRESERVICE TEACHERS USING MATERIALS CREATED TO DEVELOP THE KNOWLEDGE BASE

Kathryn Newman
Associate Professor
Grambling State University
Grambling, LA

Educators are aware of a cognitive gulf between ourselves and parents, policy makers, and even educational administrators. We seek to build partnerships, yet lack a communicative framework for dialogue. More seriously, this gulf also exists between teacher educators and preservice teachers. This is critical because preservice teachers will be taking what they perceive to be our teaching practices into classrooms and training future generations for a global economy. For example, projects, papers and even conversations with future teachers often reveal knowledge that is fragmented, or worse based merely on rote memory without the benefit of critical analysis (Levine, 1996; Tharp & Gallimore, 1989). The result is often teachers who can pass written exams (e.g., NTE or Praxis), but lack the analytical and pedagogical skills of more experienced teachers. Moreover, our own teaching methods may inadvertently reinforce this problem through heavy use of the "one question-one answer" paradigm. Teacher education programs are being mandated to produce flexible, reflective and creative teachers (e.g. Carter & Larke, 1995; Darling-Hammond, 1996; Jones-Wilson, 1996); however, the reality is that many of our strategies used to assist preservice teachers in acquiring the content knowledge may actually work against us.

Even when personnel in teacher education programs reexamine and reformulate the content and strategies students still demonstrate deficiencies. We forget that learning is a transactional communicative experience--not only must something be taught, but it must be learned. The work of Holt-Reynolds (1995) illustrates this point. On one level her preservice teacher "got it", yet on a deeper level they didn't. They comprehended the discrete elements presented to them, yet failed to grasp the ramifications of the whole. More disturbing, this failure to comprehend the entire picture is echoed in the studies of the effectiveness of "diversity" classes (e.g., Carter & Larke, 1995; Ladson-Billings, 1995) where despite passing the class, many preservice teachers did not change their essentially negative perceptions of diverse populations. Therefore, the question must be "What happened?"

Constructivist theory may provide a clue. This theory is based on the premise that all knowledge is constructed, either by the learner alone, or by the learner working with the facilitator (Spivey, 1997). Furthermore, current views that knowledge should be used as a guide (Donmoyer, 1996), not a mantra to constructing schema in education would indicate that these preservice teachers were given new knowledge, but were not assisted in analyzing how this knowledge would work in an educational setting. Consequently, I believe that teacher educators must examine the content of their teaching--not only for rigor, but also for opportunities to engage in "dialogues" with preservice teachers. These dialogues occur in the classroom, but also through interactions with the ideas presented. These outside of class dialogues are formed through the use of modified "guided notes", which form the basis for higher level cognitive processes on the part of preservice teachers. Therefore, I propose to present data from an ongoing project being used in several classes in the teacher education program that not only requires basic learning of the material, but requires students to use reflective analyses in evaluating the implications of the knowledge and selecting practices for use in their own future classrooms. Currently, preservice teachers are only required to "get the answer right", not think about it.

The theoretical framework is based upon the works of Vygotsky (1962), and Tharp and Gallimore (1989). Vygotsky (1962) examined the vast amount of learning that takes place in social contexts, and maintained that true learning cannot take place in a social vacuum. This assertion is important because if we examine the way that most teachers are trained, it is in a format far removed from most social behaviors. Specifically, it is one-sided, and requires simply rote memorization. Tharp and Gallimore (1989) examined cross-cultural perspectives. Specifically they studied how culture shapes what is transmitted, and well as how it is transmitted. They wrote that despite all of the calls for educational, teacher, and certification reforms, most teachers still teach the way that they were taught. Therefore, if teacher educators want to change the quality of future teaching, we have to change our methods as well. If we want reflective, insightful teachers who will be able to meet the demands of the 21st century educational system (e.g.,

Alley & Jung, 1995), then we have to give them opportunities to develop those reflective and evaluative skills before they get to their methods courses.

My method looks at changing one aspect of the learning process -- the quality of responses required of the learners to printed supplementary materials. Using Bloom's Taxonomy as a guide, most printed materials for preservice teachers rely heavily upon building the knowledge and comprehension components in their students. For example students learn who Piaget is, his levels of cognitive thinking, and what is expected at each age level. Few learn how to apply it, or more importantly, how to change instruction to match the cognitive level of the students to promote positive self-esteem, diversity and inclusion of all students. Preservice teachers are expected to know the names and descriptions of different types of programs for gifted students, yet few are asked to evaluate those programs for effectiveness, or choose which of the many programs would most likely match their own developing teaching style. I discovered that students who were presented with study guide materials consisting of both traditional activities and activities requiring a choice or selection by the learner were as likely to complete the latter--even though it required more work than to just pull it from the text or reading. Using the work of Craik (1973) in memory, I concluded that those activities that required not only multiple exposures and increased levels of analysis, but also reflected the personal choice of the learner would result in educational methods and materials that would be more likely to be remembered and possibly used in the real classroom setting.

The data comes from preservice teachers in our teacher education program in upper division classes. The materials examined are supplementary materials developed to enhance learning through multiple exposures to new content. Traditional supplementary materials consist of questions requiring mostly rote answers. The revised materials consist of not only knowledge and comprehension level questions, but also specific questions requiring choice and then a synthesis or evaluation of that choice. This allows students the opportunity to become more active learners as advocated by Cross and Steadman (1996). As can be seen by the samples attached that creating opportunities for informed decision making, selection of choices, and analysis of ideas presented, allows preservice teachers to demonstrate higher levels of cognitive thought as well as take on more challenging ideas.

If we are to change the type of education in the schools, we must change the education that teachers experience, especially in the teaching programs. While we may not be able to impact the size of preservice teacher classes, we can promote more of a "dialogue" of ideas by allowing preservice teachers to express and defend views, and make choices about techniques, methods and materials that they would wish to become more proficient in using. Teachers cannot be expected to teach critical thinking and analysis if they themselves have never experienced it. Teachers cannot teach learning for the sake of learning, if they have never participated in it, nor can they teach informed decision-making if all through school the decisions were made for them. Personal choice and personal investment in learning are unexplored intrinsic motivators for preservice teachers that may lead to increased numbers of teachers teaching and modeling critical thinking, as well as building communicative bridges through the active exploration of ideas.

References

Alley, R., & Jung, B. (1995). Preparing teachers for the 21st century. In M. J. O'Hair & S. Odell (Eds.), Educating teachers for leadership and change (pp.285-301). Thousand Oaks, CA: Corwin Press, Inc.

Carter, K. (1990). Teachers' knowledge and learning to teach. In W. R. Houston (Ed.), Handbook of research on teacher education (pp.291-310). New York: Macmillan Publishing Co.

Carter, N. P., & Larke, P. J. (1995). Preparing the urban teacher: Reconceptualizing the experience. In M. J. O'Hair & S. Odell (Eds.), Educating teachers for leadership, and change (pp.77-95). Thousand Oaks, CA: Corwin Press, Inc.

Craik, F. (1973). A "levels of analysis" view of memory. In P. Pliner, L. Krames, & T. Alloway (Eds.), Communication and affect: Language and thought. New York: Academic Press.

Cross, K. P., & Steadman, M. H. (1996). Classroom research: Implementing the scholarship of teaching. San Francisco: Jossey-Bass Publishers.

Cruikshank, D.R., & Metcalf, K. K. (1990). Training within teacher preparation. In W. R. Houston (Ed.), Handbook of research on teacher education (pp.469-497). New York: Macmillan Publishing Co.

Darling-Hammond, L. (1996). The quiet revolution: Rethinking teacher development. Educational leadership, 53(6), 4-10.

Donmoyer, R. (1996). The concept of a knowledge base. In F. B. Murray (Ed.), The teacher educator's handbook (92 - 119). San Francisco: Jossey-Bass.

Holt-Reynolds, D. (1995). Preservice teachers and coursework: When is getting it right wrong? In M. J. O'Hair & S. Odell (Eds.), Educating teachers for leadership and change (pp.117-137). Thousand Oaks, CA: Corwin Press, Inc.

Jones-Wilson, F. (1996). Teacher standards: "Front-burner" news again. Dialogue, 6, 1-6.

Ladson-Billings, G. (1995). Multicultural teacher education: Research, practice and policy. In J. E. Banks & C.A. Banks (Eds.), Handbook of research on multicultural education (747-762). New York: Macmillan Publishing.

59

Levine, M. (1996). Educating teachers for restructured schools. In F. B. Murray (Ed). The teacher educator's handbook (620-647). San Francisco: Jossey-Bass.

Spivey, N. N. (1997). The constructivist metaphor. San Diego, CA: Academic Press.

Tharp, R. G., & Gallimore, R. (1989). Rousing minds to life. New York: Cambridge University Press.

Vygotsky, L. (1962). Thought and language. Cambridge, MA: The MIT Press.

CHAPTER 6

ADDRESSING DEATH AND GRIEF ISSUES WITH SCHOOL-AGED CHILDREN IN A CLASSROOM GROUP SETTING

Gwendolyn Duhon-Boudreaux, Ph.D.
Assistant Professor
Department of Curriculum and Instruction
McNeese State University
Lake Charles, LA

Glenda Smith Starr, Master's +30 hours
Assistant Professor
Department of Teacher Education
Grambling State University

Nanthalia McJamerson, Ph.D.
Associate Professor
Department of Teacher Education
Grambling State University

Loretta Jaggers, Ph.D.
Associate Professor
Department of Teacher Education
Grambling State University

Mary D. Minter, Ph.D., Head
Department of Teacher Education
Grambling State University

The death of a loved one in the life of a child is one of the most traumatic experiences that they will ever encounter. When the loved one is a family member, oftentimes the children suffer more than simply the lost of the loved one. There can also be the loss of family stability and financial security. Additionally, if other family members are consumed with their own feelings of grief and loss, the children can also suffer from a lack of nurturing and emotional support normally provided by those grieving family members. In a text entitled, *Facing Death*, Wessel (1996) described a common memory shared by adults when discussing losses they suffered during their childhood:

> "When I returned home, there were lots of people around.
> Everyone was silent and weeping. No one had time for
> me. I didn't know what to do with myself. All I remember

61

is that the person I loved had disappeared and I never saw her (him) again."

Assisting children in coping with a significant loss is not a simple task. The manner of support receive by the children during the initial period of grief often determines whether or not the loss becomes an overwhelming, unmasterable burden interfering seriously with their development. If children receive the emotional support they need, they are then better able to handle their grief and integrate the coping mechanisms used into their personalities and refer back to them in future stressful situations. Mourning is a sad process for children as well as adults. It is important that adults who nurture children support and comfort them as they grieve and mourn in their own way over time. The goal is not to prevent sadness, but rather to comfort and support them in their sadness (Spiro, Curnen, & Wandel, 1996).

Children who experience the loss of an adult friend need opportunities to express their feelings and share their experiences. Towards this effort, educational practitioners (teachers, counselors, administrators) can create experiences for children to both express their grief and begin the healing process. One mechanism for initiating the process is to conduct an information-based support group that involves discussion, group processing, and an experiential activity that either reinforces the topic or provides the children with a creative outlet for the feelings generated. This is not a counseling or therapeutic group situation. The purposes of this group is to share accurate, sensitive information about death and grief, and give children an opportunity to discuss their feelings and experiences. Any child who shows evidence of needing individual counseling or professional help should be referred to the appropriate professionals immediately.

Ideally, these groups should be conducted by two adults. Having both a facilitator and co-facilitator will enable one adult to lead the discussion and the other to intervene with individual students if necessary. An entire class can participate; however, a normal group size is approximately 5-15 students. A suggested format for this type of group is as follows:

I.   Welcome: Group leaders introduce themselves and state the reasons for their visit. If students are not sitting in a circle when the facilitators arrive, the circle should be formed at that time. Once the circle is formed, the students and their teacher are asked to introduce themselves at that time.

II.   Activity: Group leaders are to inform students of the group rules. Basically, students are asked to respect each other by listening quietly when others are talking. They are also encouraged not to laugh or criticize other students during the discussion.

III.   Relaxation: Students are encouraged to stand "shake out the wiggles" before starting the discussion. Once seated again, they are asked to take a deep breath, hold it, then slowly release it. This activity is conducted to relax the students and prepare them to participate.

IV.   Discussion: The leaders discussion briefly discuss the concept of death and its finality. They can also mention some of the feelings that people sometimes experience when someone close to them dies: sadness, anger, loneliness, and numbness or a lack of emotion. The children can be asked to tell if they have experienced any of these emotions during the last few weeks by a show of hands. Next, each facilitator relates a brief remembrance of the deceased and a happy moment that they may have shared with him/her. Aterwards, they encourage the teacher to complete this task as well. Having the adults share first models the process for the students and gives them time to shape their responses. Once the adults have spoken, the children are asked to share remembrances. They are assured that they can **"pass"** when their turn to speak comes. Remind them of the rules, especially the rule against talking when another person is talking.

If any child becomes overly emotional or begins to cry, the co-facilitator should take that child out of the group and allow that child a chance compose themselves before returning to the group. If the child continues to experience difficulty, then a visit to the school counselor should be arranged.

V. Closure/Activity:

Once the children have had a chance to express themselves, the facilitators speak to children about how keeping those fond memories of the deceased will help them to deal with their feelings of grief. The facilitators will then introduce an art activity where the students draw a picture from memory of themselves and the deceased engaged in some kind of fun activity. This activity is designed to help them remember a happy occasion with the deceased and allow them to expend some energy. Before leaving the circle to begin the art activity, the facilitators will thank the children for participating in the group and close the session. The students will then return to their desks and start drawing. If the teacher, principal, and students agree, the drawings created by the students can be posted on a bulletin board as a tribute to the deceased individual.

This supportive activity can be a vehicle for the expression of feelings and a mechanism for creating dialogue. Offering students a safe and nurturing environment for sharing can make their grieving period much easier for them to handle. This can be a positive start to the grieving/healing process for children.

References

Wessel, M. (1996). When children mourn a loved one. In Spiro, H., Curnen, M. G. M., & Wandel, L. (Eds.), Facing death (pp. 34-38). New Haven, CN: Yale University Press.

Gootman, M. (1994). When a friend dies: A book for teens about grieving and healing. Minneapolis, MN: Free Spirit Publishing.

CHAPTER 7

POST-BACCALAUREATE TEACHER CERTIFICATION PROGRAMS: STRATEGIES FOR ENHANCEMENT, IMPROVEMENT, AND PEACEFUL CO-EXISTENCE WITH TRADITIONAL TEACHER CERTIFICATION PROGRAMS

Gwendolyn Duhon-Boudreaux, Ph.D.
Department of Curriculum and Instruction
Burton College of Education
McNeese State University
Lake Charles, LA

Mary Augustus, Ph.D.
Calcasieu Parish School Board
Lake Charles, LA

Rose Duhon-Sells, Ph.D.
Distinguished Professor
McNeese State University
Lake Charles, LA

Alice Duhon-Ross, Ph.D.
Assistant Professor
Albany State University
Albany, GA

Post-baccalaureate teacher certification programs (the term most commonly associated with university-based alternative certification programs) and other types of alternative certification programs became prominent in the mid to late 1980's as a mechanism to address the severe teacher shortage that existed in the academic areas of math and science, as well as in urban and rural geographic areas. In addition to filling the need for certified teachers in specific areas, Fenstermacher (1990) lists other possibilities for the acceptance of alternative certification. He believes that alternative certification:

1.   Provides opportunities for bright college graduates to begin careers in teaching without having to complete extended teacher education programs;

2.   Provides relief in times of a teacher shortage while also resolving the problems of competent performance engendered by emergency credentials;

3.   Breaks the lock that teacher education programs appears

67

to have on entry into the teaching profession;

4. Provides political capital for politicians and policymakers who want to be identified with the school reform movement;

5. Offers a means for other actors, such as foundations and corporations, to become players in the formation of teaching policy; and

6. Increases the range of choices or alternatives available for career entry, consistent with the emerging, more pervasive political ideology favoring choice and deregulation.

Through this discussion, alternative certification programs will be defined and discussed in terms of entrance requirements, length of programs, supervision and mentoring, and post-certification professional support. Strategies for improvement of alternative certification programs will be provided in the following areas:

1. Identification and building of existing alternative programmatic strengths and opportunities afforded interns to incorporate their learning experiences into their professional development; and

2. Cooperation and collaboration between alternative certification programs and traditional teacher education programs.

Definitions, Distinctions, and Descriptions

Post-baccalaureate teacher certification programs certify individual to teach through alternative routes, which vary accordingly. Some certification programs are operated by private groups and organizations, and others include those that are university-based, non-university based, and school-based. The definitions and descriptions of these various of certifying programs also vary. According to the American Association of Colleges for Teacher Education (AACTE), alternative certification may be defined as

"any significant departure from the traditional undergraduate route through teacher education programs in colleges and universities" (Smith, 1985, p. 24)

Roth (1994) defines alternative certification as certification requirements that permit demonstrated competence in appropriate subject areas gained in careers

68

outside of education to be substituted for traditional teacher training coursework. With alternative certification programs, the "alternative" part of such a program is that it gives people who already hold a college degree the opportunity to earn a teaching certificate more quickly than going through the full teacher education program. Alternative programs are geared toward mature adults, rather than college students, and vary significantly from traditional teacher education programs. Making a very basic distinction between traditional teacher certification and alternative certification, Fenstermacher (1990) asserts that the first (traditional teacher certification) requires extensive study prior to taking responsibility for a classroom, and is generally under the umbrella of a teacher education institution. The second, he states, places individuals in a classroom rather quickly, with some study and supervision, though this varies from district to district or state to state.

As stated earlier, alternative certification programs vary according to type, structure, and base of organization. Due to these differences, individuals should refrain from making sweeping generalization about the alternative programs as a whole. Roth (1994) cautions that generalizations about "alternative" programs are difficult because of the wide range of programs encompassed by the word "alternative". Some alternative programs actually provide for full preparation for certification, but through an alternative path such as flexible scheduling. Many require only limited preparation, particularly prior to assignment to a classroom. These are more appropriately referred to as alternative, since they provide an alternative set of requirements for certification, not just different means of getting there.

Similar to that of traditional certification programs, alternative programs have state standards and guidelines that vary according to their location. The National Association of State Directors of Teacher Education and Certification manual (NASDTEC, 1991) describes state standards, programs, and alternative routes to certification. The authors broadly define the term "alternative certification" and report that 34 states have 42 alternative certification avenues. Agencies administering these include combinations of the state, school districts, and colleges. Three avenues are administered solely by school districts five by school districts and the state, four by school districts and colleges, and four by school districts, colleges, and the state. A total of 11,576 candidates completed alternative avenues certification between 1988 and 1990 (NASDTEC, 1991, Q-13).

The American Association of Colleges for Teacher Education indicates that, in 1990, 48 states reported alternative-route programs for teachers leading to either permanent certification or temporary certification (AACTE, 1990). The National Center for Education Information (Feistritzer & Chester, 1992; Feistritzer, 1992) identifies 40 states implementing alternatives to the approved college teacher education program route for certifying teachers. From 1985 to 1990, approximately 20,000 candidates were certified through alternative routes. By 1992, the number had increased to about 40,000, almost doubling in two years (Feistritzer, 1992, p. 6).

Taking into consideration the variations that exist within alternative certification programs, a typical alternative program does the following things:

1.   Uses a rigorous screening process to ensure the selection of talented, qualified teacher interns who are academically and personally competent;

2.   Provides high-quality preservice training in methodology, classroom management, and human development;

3.   Consists of a structured, well-supervised induction period that includes guidance by a mentor teacher for the period of one year;

4.   Requires ongoing professional development, including seminars, workshops, and university course work that addresses the specific needs of the teacher-intern; and

5.   Follows up with post-internship training to ensure continued effective training (Littleton & Holcomb, 1994).

Colleges of education typically provide primary oversight of the programs, which are considered "field based" because they generally require a yearlong internship in the school district. That means both the school district and the university have a hand in molding the teacher intern, sharing in the professional development of the emerging teacher. This shared responsibility of the teacher-intern's professional development is accomplished through teacher induction plans. Teacher induction plans, which provide on-the-job training, are designed to help new teachers through their usually tough new year in the classroom. The university provides the preservice training, and the school district assists with the ongoing training under the guidance of a mentor teacher. The mentor, who is an experienced and fully certified teacher, serves as a guide, counselor, protector, and friend to the new teacher (Littleton & Holcomb, 1994).

With regards to the initiation of new teacher induction programs, two major categories comprise the content of these programs. One deals with the emotional trauma and addresses issues such as stress and burnout (Gold & Roth, 1993). The second provides training in the basic aspects of instruction: classroom management, discipline, lesson planning, and curriculum (Roth, 1994).

A Study in Contrasts: Texas Alternative Certification Program and Teach for America

The largest school-based teacher education effort is in Texas. The Houston Independent School District implemented the first Texas Alternative Certification Program (ACP) during the 1985-86 school year during which it prepared and certified 276 teachers. By 1989-90, 13 alternative programs had been implemented in Texas. The Board of Education revised the alternative certification rule by removing the restriction that programs be based on data verifying teacher shortages. The Texas Alternative Certification Program contains three models: the higher education model with university coursework as the nucleus of training, the education service center (ESC) model, with limited higher education supervision; and the local district model (the original model), with a minimum amount of higher education coursework. Programs emphasize preparation for the urban classroom and work with at-risk students (Roth, 1994).

This teacher preparation program has the following features:

1.   A design generated from the ground up by a broad-based coalition of educators - teachers (including former interns), principals, professors, regional service center specialists, and others;

2.   Pre-assignment training in the components deemed indispensable for entry into the classroom;

3.   A yearlong internship with a master teacher/mentor that includes inservice training and university coursework;

4.   Multiple layers of supervision and; consequently, exposure to a variety of points of view about the teaching/learning process; and

5.   A cohort group of interns who share the challenges and successes of first-year teaching and beyond (Dill, 1990).

Candidates for these programs must have a baccalaureate degree and pass a standardized test ensuring basic reading, writing, and mathematical skills.

71

Pre-assignment training occurs at night or in the summer, followed by placement as the official teacher of record in a classroom. The intern is supervised and mentored during the course of the full-year program. After a year of this internship, the new teacher must take a standardized exit or certification (ExCET) test and, if in all areas, receives the joint recommendation of the program director and the principal for state certification (Roth, 1994).

Teach for America is a non-university, private group which began in 1989 as a effort to recruit and select individuals to teach in urban and rural public schools, the areas where the teacher shortage was the most pronounced. At the onset, this organization began to train their corps members in what they considered to be a fairly traditional way. The recruits attended a series of courses and classes during a preservice summer training institute; once they began teaching, they enrolled in local schools of education to take certification courses. However, according to Wendy Kopp (1994), the group's founder and president, this approach turned out to be a frustrating one. Courses were too often disconnected from the realities of corps members' classrooms, and corps members received inadequate support and professional development after they began teaching, when they needed it most.

After their first three years, the organization began to develop their own concept of teacher education, and strong views about teacher professional development. The first was a belief that beginning teachers should assume responsibility for shaping their professional development experience. The belief stemmed from three observations:

1. Individuals learn most when empowered to exercise personal initiative and creativity;

2. The only way to ensure that professional development is relevant to classroom experience is to charge the teacher with the responsibility of shaping the professional development program; and

3. As long as teacher education treat beginning teachers as passive recipients of knowledge, alternative programs will be guilty of further socializing them into the factory-model approach to education that school reformers are working so hard to change.

A second conviction was that individuals need experience with full control over their classrooms before they can become excellent teachers. Corps members are best qualified to understand the value of professional development-and are most

72

needy of support and guidance-after they have assumed responsibility in their classrooms (Kopp, 1994).

Based on those early experiences and the group's newly developed views and beliefs about teacher education and teacher preparation, they designed a two-year "Professional Teacher Residency Program". During this time, the corps members would assume full teaching responsibility while engaged in a learner-driven professional development. What this meant for the participants was that they were given the responsibility of managing their own professional development in defined outcome areas. This development centered around their experiences. During practice teaching within the preservice program, the corps members identified challenges that they face in the classroom and weaknesses in the outcome areas. Projects were developed in order to overcome these identified challenged. As a means of assisting, an extensive support structure of guidance, resources, and opportunities for collaboration were provided to the participants. Kopp (1994) asserts that individuals should receive professional licenses to teach, not when they have taken certain numbers of credit hours, but when their teaching performance consistently demonstrated standards of excellence During the two-year internship corps members are evaluated at the end of each year and required to submit portfolios, self-evaluations, teacher work, and other documents to a review panel. Based on these documents and other information, the panel decides whether of not the participant is ready to exit the program.

The two alternative programs appear to have the same basic components: similar entrance requirements, pre-assignment training, some university coursework, and collaborative support and mentoring from participating entities. The difference lies in the philosophies: the first appears to be teacher-centered, with the emphasis on methodology, theory, and pedagogy; where the second program is more learner-centered and problem-driven. Having a strong knowledge base not only ensures success in passing the exit examination for certification, but affords interns the necessary background to address the academic needs of their students. This is a major strength of the Texas Alternative Certification Program. Knowledge of the pedagogy, methodology, and theory provides the foundation upon with effective strategies, practices, and management techniques can be built.

Conversely, with Teach for America, having the teacher-interns develop projects based on identified challenged follows the constructivist view of learning. In this approach, learners do not passively receive knowledge. Rather, they

73

"construct" it, building on the base of prior knowledge, attitudes, and values. The learner creates patterns, rules, and strategies through hands-on experimentation (Ryan & Cooper, 1995). This approach also requires the interns to bear some responsibility for their learning experience, which ensures some level of ownership in the process of their development. This may, in turn, impact their teaching styles. If they can be taught to become responsible for their learning and development as educators, then they may, in turn, require their own students to take some responsibility for their learning experiences. Requiring teacher-interns to responsibility for their learning and shifting the teacher training process from being instruction-centered (passive) to learner-centered (active) may enhance both the effectiveness of the training and the effectiveness of the interns once their step into their own classrooms.

The strengths outlined from the above mentioned programs can serve to enhance teacher preparation and effectiveness in alternative programs. Programmatic comparisons among alternative programs and between alternative programs and traditional programs also offer program directors an opportunity to observe and evaluate effective strategies that may be applicable for their programs. The one strategy that appears to stand out in the literature for enhancing alternative programs is creating collaboration between the alternative programs, university faculty and programs, schools districts, and other related parties. In a call for collaboration, Roth (1995) suggests that we:

> "...use each other's strengths. The privately funded groups could step
> up their already successful recruiting efforts and create a supply for
> schools, colleges, and departments of education. Local communities and
> schools could assist. Colleges and universities, in collaboration with local
> schools, already provide an excellent preparation for entry to the
> profession. Working together, they could provide new teachers with
> support and assistance. I truly believe this is the most beneficial
> combination, offers the best teaching environment for children, and would
> enhance the stature of the profession" (p. 264).

Kopp (1994) appeals to university schools of education to participate in collaborative efforts, asserting that they cannot develop truly effective programs without working collaboratively with school systems, recognizing and acting on their responsibility to recruit, select, and develop effective teachers. University

74

programs must look beyond their walls and forge alliances with other professions and service agencies to develop education professionals who capitalize on community resources and institutions (Roth, 1995). It appears that a shared vision among collaborating partners serves to better meet the needs of all, especially in the area of teacher training and preparation.

Conclusion

Regardless of the type alternative certification program, their primary goal is to provide competent, professionally trained teachers for America's schools. Enhancing programmatic effectiveness can be done in a number of ways, but appears to be best accomplished in cooperation with all individuals and parties involved with the certification process. As Kopp (1994) so apt put it, ..."we must work together to determine how we can realize the day when our nation's most talented individuals compete to enter the profession of teaching, and when only those whose teaching performance consistently meets standards of excellence are granted professional licenses to work alongside our nation's children" (p. 187).

References

American Association of Colleges for Teacher Education. (1990). <u>Teacher education policy in</u> the states: A 50-state survey of legislative and administrative actions. Washington, DC.

Dill, V. (1990). Support for the 'unsupportable'. <u>Phi Delta Kappan, 72</u>(3), 198-199.

Fenstermacher, G. (1990). The place of alternative certification in the education of teachers. <u>Peabody Journal of Education, 67</u>(3), 155-183.

Feistritzer, E. (1992). <u>Who wants to teach?</u> Washington, DC: National Center for Education Information.

Feistritzer, E., & Chester, D. (1992). <u>Alternative teacher certification: A state by state analysis.</u> Washington, DC: National Center for Education Information.

Grable, C., & Ogden, W. (1994). Comparison of Texas teacher appraisal system evaluations of traditional and post-baccalaureate teacher candidates. <u>Education, 114</u>(3), 470-474.

Gold, Y., & Roth, R. (1993). <u>Teachers managing stress and preventing burnout: The professional health solution.</u> London: Falmer Press.

Hawley, W. (1990). The theory and practice of alternative certification: Implications for the improvement of teaching. <u>Peabody Journal of Education, 67</u>(3), 3-21.

Kopp, W. (1994). Teach for America: Moving beyond the debate. <u>The Educational Forum, 58</u>(2), 187-192.

Littleton, M., & Holcomb, J. (1994). New routes to the classroom. <u>The American School Board Journal, 181</u>(4), 37-39.

National Association of State Directors of Teacher Education and Certification. (1991). <u>Manual on certification and preparation of educational personnel in the United States.</u> Dubuque, IA.

Smith, D., Nystrand, R., Ruch, C., Gideonese, H., & Carlson, K. (1985). Alternative certification: A positive statement of AACTE. <u>Journal of Teacher Education, 36</u>(3), 24.

Roth, R. (1994). The university can't train teachers? Transformation of a profession. Journal of Teacher Education, 45(4), 261-268.

Roth, R. (1995). Who will teach our teachers? The Educational Forum, 59(3), 258-264.

Ryan, K., & Cooper, J. (1995). Those who can, teach. Boston: Houghton Mifflin.

CHAPTER 8

"RECONSTRUCTING" LIVES:

A Reading-for-Empowerment Project

Nanthalia W. McJamerson, Ph. D.
Associate Professor
Department of Teacher Education
Grambling State University

Teacher Trainer - Grambling State University
Counselor Trainees - South Carolina State University

SUCCESS

Success "Fibers" Model Developers:
Mark Dean, Thomas Lawrence, Aprile McCullough,
Nanthalia McJamerson, Claudine Williams
South Carolina State University

Research Participants
ED 300: Educational Psychology Class
Fall 1993
Grambling State University

Project Evaluators
Katina Boden-Webb, Arlean Chistophe, Lizzie Ferguson,
Sarah Frost, Cynthia Gatson, Cassandra Lyles
Grambling State University
Carleen Riley, Harold Clarke
South Carolina State University

Project Consultants
Kathryn Newman, Ph. D., Loretta Jaggars. Ed. D.
Grambling State University

Editor
Jimmy McJamerson, M.A. + 68
Grambling State University

"RECONSTRUCTING" LIVES:

A Reading-for-Empowerment Project

Give me a dozen healthy infants, well-formed, and my own specified world to bring them up in, and I'll guarantee to take any one of them at random and train them to become any type of specialist I might select—doctor,...artist,...beggar-man and thief. (John Watson, 1925, p. 104)

If you can control a man's thinking, you do not have to worry about his actions. (Carter G. Woodson, 1993, p. 84)

There is too much failure among people who have enormous potential for success. Many of us, the teachers, parents and humanitarians, who claim that we are dedicated to helping young people, often feel powerless to solve this problem. The contention of this article is that we cannot develop solutions because we oversimplify success and overemphasize failure. Some of the popular oversimplifications are: Just believe in yourself." "Just say, 'No'." "The problem is single-parent homes." We do not seem to realize that success is not one dimensional. If we develop a deeper understanding of the multiple interactions and intricate transactions among factors which lead to success, then we can increase the possibilities for success in the lives of young people

There is a basic assumption undergirding this workbook: If we study success (Wolin and Wolin, 1994) as intensely as we study failure then we will be able to unleash the "arrested development" (Akbar, 1994) and "unbank the fire" (Hale, 1995) in the lives of young people. The workbook, therefore, was developed from the study of success rather than the study of failure.

This "RECONSTRUCTING" FAMOUS LIVES Project had as major goals an increase in our understanding of factors which lead to success and the increase of possibilities for success in the lives of project participants. The project resulted in two major outcomes. First, the "forensic" search for factors which lead to success produced the identification of essentials "fibers" for achieving success. The "fibers" are described in Figure 1. Secondly, the information about success was taught using a critical teaching approach that led to the empowerment of the project participants

Figure 1. THE SUCCESS "FIBERS" MODEL OF DEVELOPMENT

"Fibers" Essential to Successful Lives: Definitions and Assumptions

ABILITY TO NURTURE: persons or experiences which reveal, spotlight and/or nurture specific abilities, talents or capabilities in a person. Possession of ability is worthless if it is not recognized and nurtured.

AMBITION "IGNITION": exposure, event, persons which spark, develop and sustain motivation1 inspiration: purpose or propulsion in a person's life. Behind determination and endurance is ambition ignition or re-ignition. An attitude of "I want" is the antecedent of "I will".

"CARDIAC RESERVE": persons and/or experiences which cause a person to feel valuable, worthwhile or connected to others; to feel loved, cared for or important. The emotional heart must be maintained in such a ways that emotional damage can be prevented or healed. Warmth and worth, in tangent, are roots of all human behavior.

COMPETENCY TRAINING: training or instruction for competence in any area of production, expression or knowledge acquisition. Beyond schooling, competency training is the development of proficiency, virtuosity or creativity rather than mere "right-answer giving". Competence is critical for reaching one's potential.

OPPORTUNITY "RAMRODS": persons, experiences, activities or change agents which "open doors" to progress, tear down "walls" which hinder, break through "glass ceilings" or other obstructions to success. The existence of opportunities is useless to those who have no access to those opportunities.

INSIGHT "DIVIDENDS": the benefits, rewards or profit gained from awareness, raised consciousness or in-depth understanding of cognitive, social, psychological, technical and/or spiritual domains. Progress toward success is proportionate to one's amount of insight.

81

METHODOLOGY

In order to achieve the empowerment goals of the project, a critical social science approach was used. According to Shor (1980), "Humanistic methods without critical content .. .cannot help students become subjects capable of using critical knowledge to transform their world (p. 47). Therefore, qualitative methods were chosen to engage students in a process which was both emancipatory in content and liberating in process. That is, the project experience would increase participants' ability to become successful as they increase their understanding of success.

Reaching the goals of the project required a two-part design. Phase I was the in-depth study of successful lives to discern the critical factors which lead to success. This phase was conducted with four graduate counselor trainees at South Carolina State University. The group examined the autobiographies of four successful persons--Dr. Maya Angelou, Zora Neale Hurston, John H. Johnson and Malcolm X. The participants' task, during a four-week period in 1991, was to determine the critical success factors in each life. Intercoder reliability was established for the autobiographical analyses. After determining the critical success factors in each life, the group analyzed the factors to determine those factors which were common to all of the successful lives. Six essential factors or "common fibers" were identified and developed into the Success "Fibers" Model of Development (Figure 1).

Phase II of the project research was conducted during the fall of 1993, after several piloting versions of the project. Participants were asked to follow the procedures outlined in Table 1. A culminating program was produced as a result of the project. After using an experiential, emancipatory approach to the study of success, an open-ended survey was given to participants to determine the effects of the project upon them.

FINDINGS

The survey responses showed positive impact of the "Reconstructing" Lives project on all participants. Participants reported the development of a sense of empowerment in four categories: (1) increased insight, (2) increased encouragement, (3) new awareness of possibilities for personal success and (4) actual behavior changes and plan for behavior changes to create personal success.

82

FURTHER RESEARCH

As a result of the positive effects reported by project participants and by project evaluators, a workbook has been developed for use in Phase III of "Reconstructing" Lives. During the 1996-97 school year, Phase III participants took personal development pretests, engaged in the project experience and took post-tests to determine additional impact of the project in an effort to help students reach their potential.

Table 2. Trajectory - Change Statements: Insight

-"This book affected me due to the change we made (in Carson's life) in the skits. It shows how one can remove something out of a person's life and change the total outcome of that life. Ben Carson had many struggles, but something and someone was always there to the rescue. By doing this skit, it shows how every thing in life matters." (Jannard Rainey)

-"Dr. Benjamin Carson was an inspirational person who showed me that the medical profession is not "lily white" His life has also shown me how God can help you achieve. His story inspired me to also want to have a closer bond with God. Ben Carson's mother showed me what is wrong with today's children and why they are not succeeding. First, there is too much television, and secondly, there is too little motivation." (Tomirra Calahan)

-l see how people, experiences, or just one person can make a big difference in a person's life. At first, I couldn't discipline myself to read her book, but as I got into it, it became easy and enjoyable...l didn't realize that things that have happened in my life have also happened to Maya Angelou.

-l enjoyed this project and found it fun to change someone's destiny. So many times we "play life by ear" and never think about the consequences of our actions. I think that if we would think before we act sometimes, we would come out a lot better all the time.

-The project made me realize the importance of positive influences and realize I can be a positive influence in some kid's life when I start teaching.

-The study enabled me to see how to take advantage of elements of success.

-I realized how encouragement can really play a major role in a young person's life.

-I discovered I could read a whole book.

-I can relate to him and appreciate my mother's love more than before.

-This showed me an avenue to life I didn't think was too serious: "Having positive people around make a difference."

-I was better able to appreciate that success is not one-dimensional. Many factors interact to produce success.

-This project has opened my eyes to the lives of others...It also made me appreciate people in my life. I also realize without them my life would have greatly differed.

-I have "come to see" my mother differently, to appreciate her more. We can all draw inspiration from Carson's tenacity.

Table 3. Trajectory - Change Statement: Encouragement

-"The Ben Carson project affect me in Several different ways. First, reading the book.. gave me a sound perspective on success. Secondly, I got to personally know more of my classmates. Finally, reading about Ben Carson's life and his hard work actually put the spotlight on my life and how I work to get what I want. Actually, the project couldn't have come at a better time. Every semester, I'm stressed out during final week and always need to be reminded of the reason I must work hard and how it pays off in the end." (Clevoshonda Jones)

-"l always felt that as long as my parents believed in me that I will succeed, but I guess you do need outside encouragement and support. . In a society where we, African American males, are being portrayed as gang members and killers, it is truly refreshing to read about one of us who rose above that. The story should be placed in all inner-city schools so they can relate to someone who is alive and came from where they came from." (Apollos Harris)

-"In beginning, I wasn't really interested in reading the book at all. Once I began reading, I did become involved in Dr. Carson's life. The part of his life that affected me most was his spiritual belief that a higher being makes things happen--not to say that I don't believe in that same spiritual being.. .1 also believe that we are all put on this earth for a purpose and I am pleased to have read the book and will encourage others to read it also." (Sentoria Clay)

-The project gave me encouragement.

-l found encouragement and motivation in this activity.

-The project gave me a message: "Never give up!"

Table 4.: Trajectory - Change Statement: Possibilities

-"The Ben Carson study had a positive effect on me... Having positive people and things in your life can make a difference no matter how many negative things surround you...l have come to see my mother as having similar characteristics to Sonya Carson. Most can make a difference in my life; it is never too late." (Marshelia Richardson)

-"Carson affected me in many ways but most of all, he has encouraged me more to teach. Through teaching, I can be there for the "Carson" in my class. I can be there when they don't know which way to turn...,' (Dalan Sharpe)

-I still can make a difference in my life.

-I can make a difference in my future students' lives.

-I learned I have no excuse for failure.. .I can achieve my goals.

-The project showed me the possibilities for African Americans.

-I've gained insight, knowledge and intrinsic motivation...I can succeed!

Table 5: Trajectory - Change Statement: Action

-"The Carson study affected me in a very positive way. Sometimes, it is hard to believed that when you are faced with so many obstacles that it is still possible to achieve success. The Carson study inspired me to face my obstacles, head on, to overcome and even to adjust to different situations in my life for the purpose of succeeding." (Kanetra Holmes)

-The project of "Reconstructing" Lives a had profound effect on me Our project was based 0 Maya Angelou's life. As I listened to the presentations of other famous lives, I realized they all had things in common: They all had times of tragedy but prevailed in the end to become famous successful people. Doing this project made me take a closer look at my life and my children's lives. (Marilyn Warren)

-Taking a look at the lives of others has given me a chance to take a long look at my own life. I couldn't look at someone else without taking inventory on myself.. .1 enjoyed the project, and I think it will help me with my studies next year. Also, I have a greater desire now to give back to my community.

-In reconstructing the life of Nathan McCall, I learned a lot about determination and self fulfillment...l took some ideas for myself from the presentations to take a look at my own life. I have a better understanding of how people..even experiences can help shape a person's life. ...These presentations gave me some ideas on how to do my job in the future.

-The project showed me I have wasted a lot of time and prime opportunities, but I plan to change.

-1 learned to appreciate myself.. .1 was getting relaxed, but there is no time for "half stepping".

-The project caused me to start look for role models.. It gave me encouragement and determination.

References

Carson, B., & Murphey, C. (1990). Gifted hands: The Ben Carson story. New York: Harper Collins Publishers.

Glaser, B., & Strauss, A. (1967). The discovery of grounded theory: Strategies for qualitative research. Chicago: Aldine Publishing.

Shor, I. (1980). Critical teaching and everyday life. Boston: South End Press.

Watson, J. B. (1925). Behaviorism. New York: Norton.

Woodson, C. (1933). The mis-education of the Negro. New York: AMS Press.

CHAPTER 9

STUDENT EMPOWERMENT:
DEFINITION, IMPLICATIONS, AND STRATEGIES FOR
IMPLEMENTATION

Gwendolyn Duhon-Boudreaux, Ph.D.
Department of Curriculum and Instruction
Burton College of Education
McNeese State University
Lake Charles, La

Terri L. Coates, B.A.
Technical Administrator
G. T. Consultant Services, Inc.
Monroe, LA

Student empowerment and the ability of educators to empower students is fundamental to students' academic success. This paper will provide a definition of empowerment discuss the implications of student empowerment educational settings, and outline strategies for appropriate implementation of empowerment strategies.

In her article entitled *Defusing "Empowering": The what and the who"'*, Leslie Ashcroft (1987) defined empowering as "bringing into a state of belief one's ability to act effectively". Ashcroft asserted that empowering clearly embodies a principal role for the teacher in facilitating, directing, focusing, and fueling in his or her interdependent relationship with pupils. She further defined empowering as nurturing belief in capability and competence, suggesting potency and the positive impetus to action.

As indicated in Ashcroft's definition of empowerment or empowering, teachers play a crucial role in this process by the initiation and facilitation of effective relationships between teachers and students. In an article on the relationship between the perceptions of preservice teachers and minority student failure, Dr. Johanna Nel examined the type of relationship between students and teachers that serves to nurture and build self-confidence in students. She defined these relationships as "empowering relationships". She suggested that the effectiveness of these relationships in empowering students depend on the extent to which teachers:

1. incorporate students' language and culture into the culture into the school program;

2. encourage minority community participation as an integral component of children's education;

3. promote intrinsic motivation in minority students to use language actively to generate their own knowledge; and

4. become advocates for minority students in assessment procedures (Nel, 1993).

Nel's research on the importance of the student teacher relationship in minority students achievement is in close correlation to the research done by Cummins (1986, 1989) in analyzing minority students school failure. Cummins suggested that schools are failing because the relationships between teachers and students and between school and minority communities have not altered in any significant way. According to Cummins, the required changes in relationships involve personal redefinition of the way teachers interact with their students and with the communities from which the students come (Nel, 1992).

Current literature and research on student empowerment indicates the importance of students believing in themselves and teachers playing a viable role in facilitating that process by incorporating the students' cultures and languages into the program, inviting participation in the classroom by members of the students' community, and demonstrating advocacy.

In empowering students to achieve academically, teachers must also themselves feel empowered. Traditionally, schools have not empowered teachers or children. They have had little to say in the decision-making process (Stone, 1995). In her article entitled, *Empowering Teachers, Empowering Children*, Dr. Sandra Stone identified several areas in which empowering both students and teachers would improve their views of learning and work. Those areas include:

1. *Respect.* The empowered teacher is viewed as a respected professional who has the knowledge and ability to participate in the school's change. Respecting children involves recognizing and accepting who they are and what they do. Individual learning rates and styles must be respected and honored.

2. *Validation.* Validation often means sharing your knowledge of an individual's worth with someone else.

3. *Success.* We should not diminish teachers' status by focusing on weaknesses; rather we must acknowledge their strengths. Drucker

(1989) suggested that "education must focus on the strengths and talents of learners so that they can excel in whatever it is that they do well one cannot build performance on weakness, even correct ones. One can build performance only on strengths".

Respect, validation and a focus on success establishes a positive foundation for empowering both teachers and children. Stone asserted that further empowerment can be facilitated through the following methods:

1. *Ownership.* Ownership gives teachers the sense that they have as much right as administrators to make changes. Ownership for children is the feeling that the classroom is theirs, too, not just the teacher's... (Robinson, 1994);

2. *Choice.* Teachers should be able to make choices about curriculum, instructional materials, even staff. Choice for children may take many forms. They may choose what they want to study, how they will study it, which centers or projects they would like to experience, and how long they will spend on learning experiences.

3. *Autonomy.* Teachers need to be able to set their own goals and action plans, and children should be able to set their own goals and chart their own progress.

4. *Decision-making.* Empowered teachers decide what to teach, how to teach, what materials to use and how to assess students. Empowered children also make decisions that affect the classroom, including what topics to pursue and how to implement curricular choices. According to Kohn (1993), children learn how to make decisions by making decisions, not by following them.

5. *Responsible.* Empowered teachers and children become increasingly responsible for the decisions that affect their lives. As Kohn (1993) noted, "If we want children to take responsibility for their own behavior, we must first give them responsibility and plenty of it".

6. *Independence.* Stone asserted that when teachers are empowered to make their own decisions, the teachers initially exhibit high degrees of dependency. The principal's encouragement helped the teachers become independent.

7. *Risk-taking.* Empowered teachers also experience the freedom to take risks, which is important for growth and change. Empowerment releases the bonds of failure and frees children to go on learning.

8. *Collaboration.* Empowered teachers are more at ease collaborating, for they feel less of a need to compete. Empowered children also enjoy the lack of competition with others in class, and tend to be more thoughtful and cooperative.

9. *Self-evaluation.* The empowered teacher continually evaluates established goals in order to formulate new ones. Empowered children engage in self- evaluation in order to set their own learning goals.

Stone (1995) concluded by asserting that empowered teachers use support and wisdom to empower their students. Empowering children actually frees the teacher to join children in facilitating growth rather than constantly monitoring, directing and supervising the children's learning and behavior.

In a final discussion about student empowerment, this concept shouldn't be seen as something to be done during certain hours of the school day or certain periods of the school week. Ashcroft (1987) asserted that empowering is conscious and committed and pervasive or it is ineffectual and, by definition (belief, capability, effective action), therefore nonexistent. When we talk conscious, committed beliefs and pervasive, consistent, congruent theory and practice, we are talking philosophy. Empowering in schools needs to be a philosophy of education.

According to Ashcroft (1987), an empowering philosophy has several important corollarieds to note. They are.

1. Conceptions of learning as something that happens to an individual, as an internal and subjective action, as a process of inquiry and discovery;

2. Conceptions of knowledge as something that can be only be personally acquired and not given, as truths in each of us rather than as fixed and finite truths "out there";

3. Conceptions of development as personal growth, as the transformation or change of powers already present; and

4. Conceptions of classrooms as communities of learners helping each other to transform latent capabilities to active powers for the enhancement of all.

Student empowerment is crucial to the personal, intellectual, and educational growth of students. Teachers must realize their role in this process, and acquaint themselves with empowerment strategies to implement in both their classrooms and in the curriculum. They must also be aware of the correlation between their perceptions of their students and those students' academic success. Finally, in order for students to truly become empowered, the concept of empowerment must be seen as more that just another strategy for boosting academic success. It must be seen as a philosophy of education that can help students to be productive in school as well as become productive members of society.

References

Ashcroft L. (1987). Defusing "empowering": The what and the why. Language Arts, 64(2), 145-155.

Cummins. J. (1986). Empowering minority students: A framework of intervention Harvard Educational Review, 56(1), 18-36.

Cummins. J. (1989). Empowering minority students. Sacramento, CA: Association for Bilingual Education.

Drucker, P. (1989). Learning how schools must change, Psychology Today. 18-20.

Kohn, A. (1993). Choices for children: Why and how to let children decide. Phi Delta Kappan, 75(1), 8-20.

Nel, J. (1992). The empowerment of minority students: Implications of Cummins' model for teacher education. Action In Teacher Education, 14(3), 38-45.

Nel, J. (1993). Preservice teachers' perceptions of the goals of multicultural education: Implications for the empowerment of minority students. Educational Horizons 120-126.

Stone, S. (1995). Empowering teachers, empowering children. Childhood Education Annual Theme, 294-295.

Robinson, H. (1994). The ethnography of empowerment: The transformative power of classroom power. Washington, DC: Falmer.

CHAPTER 10

CHOOSING YOUR FRIENDS:
A STRATEGY FOR BEING SUCCESSFUL

Jewell L. Jackson, Ph.D.
Assistant Professor
Department of Teacher Education
Grambling State University
Grambling, LA

As we move into the twenty-first century, blacks will need to play a greater role in determining their success. As we look at past events, literature and research that focus on the positive, we find it to be somewhat limited. Therefore for the purpose of guiding young blacks, emphasis on the value of friendship cannot be overlooked. The type of friends one select can cause you to be successful or unsuccessful.

Our first focus is a scenario of who you are. You are black an adolescent, between the ages of 13 and 19. The adolescent period in your life is generally the longest period of development. It appears just after late childhood and may be tho~ght of as the transition period into early adulthood. It has also been called the "storm and stress" period in a person's life. It is during this period in your life that you will start to spend less time with family members, because your peers become increasingly important. In a study in which teenagers were paged at random intervals, it was found that these young people were in the company of age-mates for over half their waking hours. In contrast they spent only about one-fifth of their time with families (Csikszentmrhalyi & Larson, 1984).

It is common in all cultures for adolescents to have contact with each other, however, we find it much higher in industrialized counties than simpler societies. You may find yourself spending an average of 20 hours per week outside of the classroom, where as, the average teenager in Russia and Japan spend about 2 to 3 hours per week (Sarvin-Williams & Barnett, 1990). In this country we have more recreational facilities, less demanding academic standards, and the special gathering places like the video arcades, movies and the fast food restaurants. Another reason peers in other countries spend less time together is a result of them having to contribute to the family income, a sharing of tasks in the

95

household, and making preparation for their own families because they sometimes marry at a much earlier age.

Adolescents in a small hunter gatherer culture in Africa spend much of their time in very different ways from the American adolescents. For example, Kikuyur adolescents in central Kenya spend two-thirds of their waking hours in chores and family malntenance tasks (Munroe & Others, 1984). Girls of rural India spend a similiar two-thirds of their time malntenance tasks, including 1 1/2 hours fetching water, while boys spend two-thirds of their time in leisure (Sarasivathi & Dutta, 1988). Contemporary Japanese adolescents spend well over half their waking hours doing schoolwork. How adolescents spend their waking hours provides insight into the nature of their developmental experiences in a culture and the crrcumstances that influence what women and men will become (Larson & Richards, 1989).

Even before specific friendships are created, the peer group serves many purposes. It first serves as a bridge between the family and your entering into adult roles. At this point in your life, social roles are important for success become there are many social skills that must be mastered for psychological growth. This group also provides emotional support as you advance toward maturity.

In order to be successful or even advance toward success, it is very important that you understand the difference between friendship, your peer group and cliques that sometimes you are caught up with. Being a part of the aforementioned and not understanding your real role can cause many problems that can hinder your success. It is not uncommon for black students to get the three confused which creates further complications for you.

Most of your peer group relations during this period in your life can be categorized in one of three ways: individual friendship, the cliques, and the crowds.

Individual friendship: this is the smallest of the three groups, generally four to six person in your early teens to about two in your late teens. These are the persons that are considered to be most trusted with a type of psychological closeness and mutual understanding. They are usually similar in age, sex, race, and social class. Friends are also alike in attitudes and values, such as educational aspirations, political beliefs and are usually willing to try some of the same deviant behavior. It is interesting to note that most of your friends live in similiar neighborhoods that maybe somewhat segregated by income, race and belief systems.

The clique: A clique is a small group of about five to seven members who are either close or good friends. These members are usually alike in age, race, and social class. In the early teen years cliques are generally same sex members, but in the late teen years, it is not uncommon for them to be mixed-sex groups.

The crowd: The crowd is a large loosel~ organized group consisting of several cliques. Unlike the clique, the crowd grants you an identity within the large social structure of the school or community. Toward your late teen years, the crown declines in importance. By this time your should have acquired new social skills and have your own personal values that will be geared for your success.

During your adolescent years, you will under go many important charges. This period is quite different form childhood when you were included in all of the playground activities in your school. many times you were palred by the teacher and included in the games and other activities. However, as your move through the teenage years, you may find yourself being overlooked, or worse yet. being disliked and rejected by classmates or other associates. It is during this period that cliques, or crowds take on a more important role as your began to "hang out". It is during this time that you will also find out how important it is to have a smaller number of friendships that are more intense and more intimate.

Benefits of Friendship

You might ask yourself what benefits will I gain from my friends? Close friends and other peers are primary partners in your social interactions. You are probably aware of the amount of time that you spend talking to your friends, either in person or on the telephone. Actually, you spend more time talking to peers than any other single activity. Close friendships during your teenage years are definitely related to many aspects of your psychological health and competence. Friendship further helps with your social and emotional development. The benefits of friendship can be summarized in three categones:

1.   Close friendship provide opportunities to explore the self and develop a deep understanding of others. Through open, honest communication, adolescent friends become sensitive to each other's strengths and weaknesses, needs and desires. They get to know themselves and their friends especially well, a process that supports the development of self concept, perspective taking, identity an intimate ties beyond the family (Sullivan, 1983).

2. Close friendship help young people deal with the stresses of the adolescence period. Friendships enhances sensitively to and concern for another, it also increases the likelihood of empathy and prosocial behavior. It has been reported that teenagers with supportive friendships report fewer dally hassle and more "uplifts" than do others (Kanner et al., 1987). As a result, anxiety and loneliness are reduced while self-esteem and sense of well-being are fostered.

3. Close friendships can improve adolescents attitudes toward school. Teenagers with satisfying friendships tend to do well in school. The link between friendship and academic performance depends, if course, on the extent to which each friend values achievement (Epstein, 1983). It has also been found that friendship ties promote good school adjustment in both middle and low-income students. When teenagers enjoy interacting with friends at school, perhaps they begin to view all aspects of school life more positively (Savin-Williams and Berndt, 1990).

Research yielded much of the information presented. Therefore, you should be able to relate to the impact of friendship during your teen years and strive hard to be successful.

Appropriate and inappropriate strategies for making friends.

Let's look at your behavior as being appropriate or inappropriate for generating positive or negative responses from your peers. It is important for you to understand what is appropriate and what is inappropriate if you want to make a hit and generate friendships that will benefit you now and later in life.

A. Appropriate Strategies for making friends:

1. Initiate interaction
   a. Learn about friends: do such things as ask their names, ages, and favorite activities.
   b. Make personal overtures: Introduce yourself, start a conversation, invite them to do things.
2. Be Nice: Make a practice of just being nice, kind and considerate.

3. Exhibit prosocial behavior
   a. Be honest and trustworthy: tell the truth and keep promises,
   b. Be generous, cooperative and share
4. Have respect for self and others.
   a. Be polite, courteous, and listen to what others have to say.
   b. Have a positive attitude and personality. Be open to others, be friendly and use humor.
   c. Be yourself. Enhance your own reputation by being clean, neat and exhibit your best behavior.
5. Provide social support
   a. Be supportive by giving help, good advice and show you care.
   b. Engage in activities together. Find time to study or play. Sit next to one another.
   c. Enhance others by complimenting them.

Just as there are appropriate behaviors for making friends, there are also inappropriate behaviors that will cause you to lose friends and become less desired by others. The following are inappropriate for making friends.

B. Inappropriate behaviors:
1. Psychological aggression
   a. Show disrespect by exhibiting bad manners: be prejudiced, inconsiderate, use others, curse and be rude.
   b. Be illusive and uncooperative by ignoring and isolating them. Never invite them to do things or share.
   c. Hurt their reputation or feelings by spreading rumors, gossiping, criticizing and finding ways to embarrass them.
2. Negative self-presentation
   a. Be selfcentered, snobby, conceited and jealous. Try to show off on your friends and care only about yourself.

b. Exhibit meanness and exhibit a bad attitude at all times. Act cruel and hostile.

c. Hurt your own reputation by being stupid, throw temper tantrums and start trouble.

3. Antisocial Behavior

a. Exhibit physical aggression by fighting, tripping others and causing physical harms.

b. Show verbal aggression that is out of control. Yell at others, pick on them, call them names and just be plain bossy.

c. Be dishonest and disloyal by telling lies, stealing, cheating, break promises and tell secrets.

d. Break school rules by skipping school, drinking alcohol and using drugs.

Sullivan (1953) contended that friends are needed for well being because people have a number a basic social needs including the need for tenderness, attachment, playful companionship, social acceptance and intimacy. The fulfillment of these needs may be through the use of appropriate or inappropriate behavior. However, if you as a teenager are to be successful, you will need to understand what is appropriate and shun the behaviors that are labeled as inappropriate.

What Black Students Disclosed about Selecting Friends

A Human Growth and Development class of freshman black students were asked to write two to three paragraphs on how the selection of friends has caused them to be successful or unsuccessful thus far. The findings were very interesting and are shared here in a series of summary statements. The statements follow:

1. I choose my friends very carefully because you can't trust everyone. (D.S.)

2. My friends and associates haven't affected me because I use my own mind. (M.C.)

3. Friends have a positive and negative affect on you. They can affect the things you do and say (S.T.)

4. I have associates but very few friends because I found out the hard way they can have influence and power over you. (J.J.)

100

5. I don't let anyone control me or pressure me into doing anything that goes against my morals and values. (M.M.)

6. A friend is a person that is there for me when I need them. (R.R.)

7. I only select people that are trustworthy and dependable. (R.R.)

8. I know very few people that I can label as a friend. (R.R.)

9. Friends are hard to find because most people are not to be trusted. (I.W.)

10. The experiences of several cultures have helped me be successful to this point. (I.W.)

11. I don't have many friends because this keeps me out of trouble. In the past I had dealings with gangs. We smoked weeds and did a lot of drinking. (R.J.)

12. Friends don't let you down nor deal with hearsay. (K.J.)

13. My old friends got me in trouble so now I find out about people before I go hanging around. (K.J.)

14. I would have failed some of my classes if I hadn't made friends. It's good to have someone to talk to instead of keeping everything to yourself. (K.J.)

15. My selection of friends are very few because of some bad experiences in the past. (S.T.)

16. I found that God is my only true friend. (S.T.)

17. I have only one friend in which I trust and have faith in. (S.J.)

18. My selection of associates in the past helped me be unsuccessful because I was caught in some of the bad things they were doing. (S.B.)

19. My past selection of friends have caused me to be both, successful and unsuccessful. (L.H.)

20. The best friends I have is myself because my past friends are nothing but trouble. (L.H.)

21. A friend is someone you can trust, respect and get along with. (F.M.)

It is very apparent that this group of students learned much from trial and error and some of their previous experiences have left them somewhat skeptical. However, if they had been exposed to appropriate and inappropriate strategies for making and selecting friends, they could have been spared some painful lessons they learned as they progressed through high school.

Hopefully, after examining this chapter, you will be prepared to use this information to make yourself a successful black student.

"Each friend represents a world in us, a world possibly not born until they arrive, and it only by this meeting that a new world is born."

Anais Nin

References

Csikszentrnihalyi, M., & Larson, R. (1984). Being adolescent. New York: Basic Books.

Larson, R., & Richards, M.H. (1990). Introduction: The changing life spare of early adolescence. Journal of Youth and Adolescence, 18, 501-509.

Monroe, R. H., Himmin, H.S., & Munroe, R.L. (1984). Gender understanding and sex-role preferences in four cultures. Developmental Psychology, 20, 673-682.

Santrock, J. W. (1995). Life-span development. Dubuque, IA: Brown and Benchmark.

Saraswathi, T., & Dutta, R. (1988). Invisible boundaries: grooming for adult roles. New Delhi, India: Northern Book Center.

Sarvin-Williams, R.C., & Berndt, T.J. (1990). Friendship and Peer Relations. In S.S. Feldman & G.R. Elliot (Eds.), At the threshold: The developing adolescent. Cambridge, MA: Harvard University Press.

Sullivan, H.S. (1953). The interpersonal theory of psychiatry. New York: W.W. Norton.

CHAPTER 11

A COMMON SENSE APPROACH FOR MANAGING CLASSROOM DISCIPLINE: A PRACTICAL GUIDE FOR FIRST-YEAR TEACHERS

Elaine Foster, M.Ed.
Assistant Professor
Department of Teacher Education
College of Education
Grambling State University
Grambling, LA

Silence hovers over the third grade classrooms the teacher explains the inter-related steps of long division. Student attention is fixated on the lesson development and mastery is evidenced with the correct responses given. The lesson unfolds and the learners independently solve problems, carefully following each step. Is this a vivid description of your class or do you find yourself constantly interrupting the lesson to reprimand off-task behaviors that deter the lesson sequence and hinder the accomplishment of the lesson objectives?

Many novice teachers are faced with the escalating challenge of effectively managing disruptive classroom behaviors. They enter the teaching profession with a plethora of content knowledge but with limited competency-based discipline skills. Theoretic and academic-based methods courses do not provide pre-service teachers with sufficient knowledge and application of these skills. Competency based discipline skills are usually acquired with on the job experience after an influx of inappropriate behaviors have been exhibited by students.

In 1994, the Louisiana House of Representatives initiated Concurrent Resolution 7 which urged and requested that the Board of Regents, the three higher education management boards, and the public colleges of education take all measures necessary to create a course for pre-service teachers to identify and respond to students with serious disciplinary problems and to make such course mandatory for graduation from a teacher training program. This legislation led to the realization of the need for all preservice teachers to become competent and effective classroom disciplinarians. The American public views lack of discipline as being one of the major problems faced by local public schools. and their outcry is for this issue to be addressed at every level so that maximum learning can occur in all educational settings. National Educational Goal Number Seven emphasized that every school in the United States should offer a disciplined environment conducive to learning, by the year 2000. As we stand on the threshold of the new millennium, it is imperative that novice teachers become equipped to meet these national and local demands that require them to be able to properly respond to off-task behaviors.

An insight to the dynamics of human behavior is vital in assisting novice teachers with formulating a course of action for altering or diminishing target behaviors. The "what", "why", and "how" of human behavior must be taken into consideration. What is the inappropriate behavior exhibited by the student? Why is the student exhibiting this behavior? How can I change this behavior? The responses to these questions can greatly influence the selection of an intervention and the effectiveness of the interaction. All behavior has antecedents and consequences. Being cognizant of factors that contribute to existing target behaviors can provide the foundation for the conceptualization of alternatives that intensify behavior modifications.

The most competent teachers sometimes experience disruptive classroom behaviors. Knowing what to do and how to do it, is the key to achieving classroom harmony and to assuring that the method(s) used will be effective and have a salient affect on students. There is no simple solution to school discipline and there is no single behavior management program that can prescribe the formula for decreasing inappropriate behaviors and increasing target behaviors. However, a common sense approach to classroom management can be successfully implemented to alter diverse behaviors through the eclectic selection of components from the continuum of classroom management systems. The continuum serves as a catalyst for selecting strategies that can be modified to create tailor-made techniques that enable novice teachers to reduce and eliminate specific student behaviors. A broad spectrum of strategies for modifying behaviors fall between the categories of self-discipline which include: Maslow's hierarchy of needs, William Glasser's reality therapy, Thomas Gordon's teacher effectiveness training, Jacob Kounin's desist strategies, Lawrence Kohlberg's moral reasoning, Lee Canter's Assertive Discipline, and B. F. Skinner's behavior modification.

The common sense approach to classroom management affords the teacher the liberty to conceptualize a modification technique utilizing the theoretical concepts presented at the broad and narrow ends of the spectrum of imposed

106

discipline and self-discipline. The teacher's knowledge of each student's physiological traits increases the probability of selecting strategies from the continuum that are best suited for altering individual target behaviors. Acknowledgment of individual differences is vital when selecting strategies that yield the most effective results. Students are different, behaviors are different, therefore it is necessary to incorporate a variety of management techniques that can redirect behavior with long-term results. Effective teachers realize that facilitating learning rests upon the effective use of management techniques.

This approach employs a three step procedure that accentuates the selection of a target behavior, the eclectical selection of management techniques from the continuum and integration and application of the components of specific behavior management techniques. These techniques can be customized to modify off-task behaviors and to maintain desirable behaviors.

Identifying the target behavior is the initial step in the behavior change process. The target behavior is the behavior in need of modification. It may be an existing behavior or a covert behavior. A covert behavior may be one that is not observable in the individual's behavioral repertoire but one to be developed. It is prevalent for a classroom teacher to identify a variety of target behaviors because all children manifest behaviors that are unacceptable to some other individual under various conditions. A teacher may recognize the following behaviors:

1. verbal outburst
2. inattentiveness
3. incomplete homework assignments

All of the above are potential target behaviors that can be observed in the classroom. Target behaviors may be exhibited by a individual student or an entire class. The key element is for the teacher to select a target behavior based on set criteria instead of indiscriminately selecting a behavior that does not compel a modification technique. Foresight should be given to the following questions when selecting a target behavior:

1. What kind of behavior is evident?
2. What is the frequency of the behavior?
3. What is the duration of the behavior?
4. What is the intensity of the behavior?

The responses to these questions can provide the teacher with a baseline for creating a technique that successfully augments or contracts the target behavior.

The continuum of management strategies is comprised of seven highly effective theoretically based self-discipline and improved discipline modification systems. It is imperative that the novice teacher develops a global conception of these management systems and how to integrate the components for the successful design and implementation of the customized technique to be used for the alteration of classroom behaviors that displace the regular routine and impede the learning process. You cannot implement a system on "the spur of the moment". Systems must be studied and analyzed.

Self-discipline strategies focus on positive teacher expectations and encompass the following:

1. Maslow's Hierarchy of Needs (physiological needs, safety needs, love and belonging needs, esteem needs, and the need for self-actualization). Fulfillment of these needs can be considered a determinant of behavior.

2. Kohlberg's Theory of Moral Reasoning (preconventional morality, conventional morality, and post-conventional morality). These hree levels of moral reasoning emphasize acceptable and unacceptable behavior at school and provide explicit reasons that explain why certain behaviors cannot be tolerated. As a student progresses through each stage of moral development, perspective taking increases thus creating heightened perception of what is right and what is wrong.

3. Teacher effectiveness training is a strategy built on the premise that the teacher and students can effectively resolve classroom conflicts altogether by adhering to these steps:
   a. describe the problem
   b. explore possible solutions
   c. assess the solutions
   d. determine the best solution
   e. implement strategies
   f. create evaluation plan

4. Reality therapy involves the teaching of individual responsibility utilizing a realistic approach that guides the student toward redirecting his/her behavior. This technique employs seven principles which includes:
   a. direct student and teacher interaction;

b. a focus on current behavior;

c. examining the current behavior, evaluating it, and determining if the current behavior is appropriate or inappropriate;

d. student and teacher developing a plan to help meet personal goals;

e. a written commitment from the student to maintain and fulfill the plan;

f. accepting no excuses when the student fails to change the behavior; and

g. absence of punishment. This technique requires the student to become accountable for maintaining appropriate behavior.

The dominant source of authority in the classroom lies within the teacher. The teacher's authority is defined as the legitimate use of power as recognized by society, that is by parents, school administration, courts, legislatures, and students. Violation of the power of authority may necessitate the application of an imposed discipline strategy. These strategies assist in the restoration of authority to the teacher utilizing desist strategies, assertive discipline techniques, and behavior modifications.

Desist strategies assimilate three levels of force that range from low to high and may be executed publicly as privately. Low desist is always nonverbal and gestural. It may be a stern glance or shaking of the head to indicate to the student that his/her behavior is unacceptable and immediate cessation behavior is necessary. Moderate desist is invariably verbal and requires the teacher to express to the students the necessity to behave appropriately. High desist employs verbal and nonverbal reactions in response to the off-task behavior. A verbal reprimand and coercion may be used to retrieve the desired behavior.

Behavior modification is an approach that challenges the teacher to adhere to the following steps in the behavior change process:

1. select the target behavior,
2. select and record the baseline data,
3. identify reinforces,
4. implement intervention,
5. collect and record intervention data,
6. evaluate the effects of the intervention.

109

The continuum functions as a scaffold for the neophyte teacher. Components from each management system can be linked to procreate a technique specifically tailored to increase or decrease target behaviors. The facilitation of learning is contingent on the successful implementation of diverse management techniques that exhibit saliency. The most effective system can be your own creation.

References

Johnson, J., & others. (1994). Introduction to the foundations of American education (9th ed.). Boston: Allyn and Bacon.

Ormrod, J. E. (1998). Educational psychology: Developing learners (2nd ed.). Upper Saddle River, NJ: Prentice Hall.

CHAPTER 12

REGIONAL AND LOCAL PARTNERSHIPS IN TEACHER EDUCATION

William Njume Ekane, Ph.D.
Associate Professor
Department of Teacher Education
College of Education
Grambing State University
Grambling, LA

ABSTRACT

The new challenges facing teacher education, teacher trainers, and in-service teachers in the twenty-first century in Africa are enormous. These challenges are due to drastic changes in rapid population growth; explosion of knowledge; explosion of aspirations; a systematic bias against human development in public expenditures; education that is buffeted by conflicting currents; from laissez-faire individualism to overcentralization of decision-making; managerial inefficiency and curriculum adaptation as opposed to curriculum reconstruction; and a conspicuous absence of partnership in the educational enterprise. This paper, presented at the International Society for Teacher Education (ISTE) Seminar held at The University of Buea, Buea Cameroon, Africa, 20th - 26th April, 1995, attempts to address the above issues and propose a model that will enable teacher education to face the twenty-first century with greater preparedness and certainty.

INTRODUCTION

Education in both the developed and developing countries is generally perceived as an elixir for the many social ills plaguing the nations of the world. This is more so because education is viewed by many as the primary instrument in social upward mobility and economic development. Teacher education ought therefore to serve as the base from which well-trained teachers should be able to transform the educational system created under the colonial era.

But the reality of teacher education today in many countries in Africa is that it does not reflect the growing needs of the population. Teacher education is left primarily in the hands of government agencies instead of being tackled as a shared responsibility between parents, teachers. the community and specialists in child upbringing (Chapman & Taylor 1970). Furthermore, the new challenges facing teacher education today are knowledge explosions, explosion of aspirations, rapid population growths, overcentralization of decision-making, managerial inefficiency, curriculum reconstruction and lack of partnership in educational enterprise.

The previous problems pose significant and compelling demands on any single teacher education program. Therefore we envisage that if teacher education programs at the pre-service and in-service levels are run in a co-operative manner, the school systems will meet the expectations of developing appropriate skills, knowledge and attitudes for the development of the African nations.

Why Partnership?

The forces demanding change in education are basically four, the student, parents, teachers and society. For meaningful change to be brought about, we need the consultation and partnership of these forces for the following reasons:

(i) *Lack of collaboration:*

Changes in the administrative organization of education will need to provide a solution to the problem of poor coordination of educational programs and activities as well as a solution to the problem of dualism in educational responsibilities, in order to bring about greater co-ordination among the divergent controlling agencies of education.

`Also, with the economic liberation and democratization process in Africa, many schools and institutions are being built by government, voluntary agencies and other private organizations and by individuals. Often the coordination of programs and educational activities undertaken by these agencies is weak, particularly as regards the type of curriculum and infrastructure set up in the schools.

(ii) *Difficulties of communication.*

Bureaucracy and overcentralization in many African countries tend to stifle initiatives particularly at the local level. (UNECA, 1994). Often the process of curriculum development, implementation and evaluation is slowed down which

114

in turn affects the rate of curriculum development and implementation. The centralized education system presents enormous communication difficulties in obtaining feedback from schools about curriculum implementation and evaluation.

Even at the local level itself, the lack of contact and communication among teachers leaves many schools guessing what might be going on in school premises. As Beard et al, (1984) remark, teachers have by and large lived and worked in isolation from their colleagues and counterparts for too long. They need to know specific information about relevant merits and intensive work carried out in other disciplines.

It is therefore imperative that open lines of communication between teachers within the local schools as with teachers from outside the local region be established. It is equally important to realize that lack of communication can lead to a lot of waste and duplication by the managers of education.

(iii) *Need for Decentralization:*

A reorientation of education to development needs should be accompanied by decentralization of its administration. For example, decisions concerning the governance of teaching as a profession are carried out by higher education authorities, usually without seeking the teachers' opinion in areas such as the recruitment of teachers, types of teacher training, the subjects offered, time allocated to each subject and the selection of pupils/students. In addition, textbooks are often prescribed for them, they cannot change them, and the methods of assessing student progress are also prescribed. Even in the classroom a teacher has many handicaps in making decisions. Many decisions are already made for him before he enters the classroom (e.g. rigid rules, prescribed instructions and the popular teachers' guides). When teachers are not made equal partners in the educational process they are often restricted from maneuver and making independent decisions that might better serve the students. (UNECA, *1994).* Partnership in decision-making will strengthen regional and local services. Delegating the needed authorities to such regions or local agencies as well as to school levels will enhance curriculum implementation.

(iv) *Pooling of Resources:*

The contemporary teacher faces the difficult task of equipping students to cope with the diverse changing and challenging needs of the community through programs that emphasize the integration of theory with practice. In addition, the teacher trainer has the arduous task of designing and implementing new delivery

115

strategies using state-of-the-art technologies to accommodate large classes. He also needs to design a value-oriented education suited for complete human development and responsible citizenship in the contemporary world (Ekane, 1992). "In sum, the student -teacher ought to be taught to work in difficult conditions from those he is used to, to think productively, read intelligently and exercise proficiency in his respective areas of specialization." (Ekane, 1993).

Furthermore a pooling of human resources and experiences would surely be of great value in this partnership between managers of education enterprises. It is a fact that many well-conceived development projects in African states have often not been implemented for tack of funding. In order to establish effective partnership among the agents of education, funding is needed. Such funding could be obtained from private individuals, government organizations as well as non-governmental organizations and private donors.

After highlighting the importance of partnership in the previous pages, this paper will identify areas of partnership in teacher education. Firstly, cooperation should take place at the Pre-service level and secondly at the in-service level.

Before we get into a detailed discussion of the pre-service and in-service programs of teacher education, this paper proposes a model (in the form of an organigram) which will facilitate and promote collaboration at the local as well as at the regional levels.

At the local level, this author proposes the creation of a Provincial Teacher Pedagogic Center (PTPC), a Divisional Teacher Pedagogic Center and at the national level, a National Teachers Pedagogic Center (NTPC). At the Regional level, this paper also proposes an African Regional Teachers Pedagogic Center (ARTPC). It is important to note that Region here stands for the African continent. Under the aegis of ARTPC the following broad goals could be pursued.

A.) Setting the structures of ARTPC;

B.) Coordinating the functioning of the NTPC.

Under (A) above we propose that a governing board and its secretariat be created. This governing body would constitute, one member from a Teacher Training College designated by each government of each African state, a vice-chancellor of a university
from each African state and another member nominated by each government from the public service.

In this way, both the political agenda of government and academic interests of Teacher Training Colleges would be addressed. At both the local and

116

national levels, each country would set-up sub-committees whose representatives would consist of parents, teachers, specialist, administrators in the Ministry of Education and representatives from public and private corporations.

Fig. 1 on page 7 is a paradigm that portrays partnership and relationships at the Local1 National and Regional levels.

Fig 1: Partnership in Teacher Education in Africa

ARTPC

NTPC   NTPC   NTCP

PTPC   PTPC   PTPC

DTPC   DTPC   DTPC

ARTPC-   African Regional Teacher Pedagogic Center
NTPC-   National Teacher Pedagogic Center
PTPC-   Provincial Teacher Pedagogic Center
DTPC-   Divisional Teacher Pedagogic Center

At the Divisional and Provincial Teacher Pedagogic Centers, decisions about inservice teacher education programs will be treated as well as other issues in education at their respective levels. where necessary there will be on going dialogue between the DTPC, PTPC and NTPC so that there is a constant flow of information.

Decision reached at DTPC, PTPC will be communicated to NTPC and vice versa. The model is designed so that information flows from top to bottom and vice versa.

A major function of the ARTPC might be the creation of a clearing-house for current research on Teacher education in Africa. The findings of such works would be published. Also, scholarly work carried out in the different countries and solutions found in certain areas of common interest should be forwarded to ARTPC for dissemination.

Funding for ARTPC to start work could easily be obtained by first identifying and clearly articulating the needs and goals of the board to local governments and international organizations (like UNESCO or other private organizations that are interested in supporting the efforts of Teacher Education in Africa). Another short term goal of ARTPC could be to set up an ad hoc committee that will gather information on all African Teacher Training Colleges -- their programs and structures so as to come up with a handbook in African Teacher Training Colleges.

Out of the work of the ad hoc committee of ARTPC could emerge collaboration in (B) above, in the areas of pre-service and in-service programs of the respective countries in Africa.

Pre-Service Teacher Education Programs

The ultimate goal and objectives of education and economic considerations directly affect teacher training. All Teacher Training institutions should therefore produce teachers who are able to guide pupils/students towards adulthood by making them independent thinkers and capable of finding solutions to their own problems. Unfortunately, this is not the case as UNECA remarks,

> "Both at the levels of theory and practice teacher
> education is characterized by confusion, effervescent
> hopes, mordant fears, wishful thinking and increasing
> pessimism" (UNECA, 1994)

In order to reverse the extant trends in teacher education, cognizance of objectives of teacher education must conform with national policy on the development of education in each country. Provision must be made to ensure that educational opportunities are open to all shades of society though formal and

119

non-formal educational programs in literacy, numeracy, basic knowledge, and practical skills.

Also the curriculum must stress the art of teaching which includes among other things helping the pre-service teacher to be able to teach the students the techniques of probing, discovering, analyzing problems and maximizing activities to ensure the development of right attitudes , values and the more straight forward tasks of skill development.

The curricula in the Teacher Training colleges should be re-examined to ensure that:

(i)   What is taught in colleges is immediately transferable to the classrooms when the pre-service teacher graduate;

(ii)   There is enough time for practicums.

At the national level, the NTPC should hold regular meetings to discuss and come up with solutions to such urgent problems faced by the training colleges. UNECA (1994)~ catalogues some of these issues:

(i)   Lack of adequate infrastructure, equipment, textbooks3 laboratories and

sometimes qualified teachers to teach in these training institutions.

(ii)   Inadequate supervisors by subject specialist during teaching practice. Many students are supervised by non-subject mentors.

(iii)   Qualities of teachers or mentors at school where students are placed varies greatly from one school to another, often very little help is given to the student. Sometimes there is little help offered because some classroom teachers lack experience themselves.

(iv)   Prospective teachers ought to be given help or experience on how to get learners motivated because quite often educational method courses do very little in this domain.

(v)   Teacher education to date continues to impart information on teaching the common disciplines. This problem is still with us today. (Tanner & Tanner, 1980). Therefore our expectations of prospective teachers as well as teachers in the field continues to be unrealistic in view of the kind of preparation they receive and the kind of assistance they get when out on the job. In order to produce the type of teachers society desires and if educational opportunities for learners are really to be improved, an adequate education of

120

teachers must include curriculum development (both theory and work of curriculum development).

(vi)   In some teacher education programs, elementary education is divorced conceptually and administratively from secondary education. This segmented view of education mitigates against considerations of the curriculum as a continuous growth. There is also the need to conceptualize pre-service and in-service teacher education as an unbroken continuum.

In-service Teacher Education Programs

No single teacher training program, no matter how good and how long it last, will adequately keep a teacher abreast and intellectually active in a world of increasing changes in the field of education. Curriculum changes, new knowledge and modem teaching technologies require that serving teachers must be given continuing opportunities for learning and in-service training.

Such in-service activities can be undertaken in various forms; seminars, workshops, colloquies, short-term internships, and exchange visits to other places, just to mention these. Some of these activities are carried on by and large in various countries but a major problem identified by Tanner and Tanner (1980) is that teachers who implement curriculum in schools are not involved in curriculum conceptualization, design, and development. Teachers supposedly make crucial decision about what is to be taught and how it is to be taught. The most important thing to understand clearly is that curriculum improvement depends on teachers. It is in this respect that this paper calls for partnership especially at the local and national levels, because there is no provision for decision-making by teachers. Teachers are expected to be architects of core curriculum although administrators fail to provide them with the needed materials, consultative help and supportive conditions for teacher development. Teachers must play a role in generating knowledge about the curriculum. Teachers who participate actively in curriculum revision bring new intelligence in their teaching. In sum, teachers should be developed as professionals not technicians, since technicians only implement decisions whereas professionals have broad discretionary powers in decision making.

In order to make the foregoing idea, more practical reference will be made to the proposed Teacher Resource Centers in the model in Figure 1.

At local level (i.e. DTRC & PTRC) teachers should be encouraged to take responsibility for curriculum development. These Teacher Resource Centers could also serve to:

-focus teacher interest on new ideas in education;

-treat problems facing teacher education;

-focus on practical, in-service education through courses, lectures, workshops and dissemination of curriculum techniques, novel methods of teaching and the production of teaching aids;

- discuss issues about their profession (this is more of a social function to combat loneliness and demoralization);

- converse on and be intelligent consumers of research.

According to Foshay, the responsible act of teaching requires that the teacher "draws on what is known of educational practice and gather evidence in some coherent way, The ability to synthesize this knowledge in action is the hallmark of the professional teacher". (p 224).

In the goal of furthering meaningful partnership for the in-service teacher, the author identifies three enormously important resources for problem-solving. They are time, expertise and materials.

Time: Teachers should be encouraged to work in groups especially team-teach. In this way, they will serve as support to each other. Teachers must also be provided blocks of time on a monthly basis for deliberation in schools as well as in resource centers to identify substantial problems and develop plans for actions to attack the problems.

Expertise: In each Divisional and Provincial Teacher Resource Center, there should be consultative help available for teachers. Supervisors and peers should also be available to assist teachers on invitation, responding to the teacher's expressed needs. Universities have a vital role to play in this regard; school-university cooperation programs for curriculum development can be enormously effective.

Furthermore from the literature and professional organizations, principal and teachers can identify schools that are trying out new curriculum designs and materials. They should send task forces to explore the success and efficiency of using these approaches in the local schools, and they should inform Provincial, National and Regional Teacher Resource Centers.

122

Materials: It is imperative that teachers must have didactic materials to improve learning. One wonders how much of the educational budgets is allocated to purchase materials such as textbooks, teaching-aid, tools, library books, curriculum materials and other instructional materials.

It is recommended that at the local level, the governments that own educational institutes allow a free-hand for DTRC and PTRC to solicit funds, produce materials such as books, pamphlets and didactic materials, sell and manage the finances as the subcommittee made up of (parents, teacher administrators) deem fit. These ideas will empower the resource centers, promote ownership and foster initiatives. Another possible major area of fruitful partnership lies in the professional relationship between administrators and teachers. Of profound importance for teachers' involvement in curriculum development is the nature of teacher relationships with administrators and supervisions. The kind of relationship between teacher, principal and field inspectors (Divisional, Provincial, and National Inspectors) is a contributing factor to impeding curriculum improvement. Supervisors generally tend to be error oriented. In their task of supervision they only point out teachers' errors. In our opinion this does not give professional standing to teaching. At times reports are made about the in-service teachers teaching performance without discussing the observations with the teachers concerned.

Very clearly then. the criticism of teachers by their supervisors must be followed up with suggestive help. Also, improving the curriculum depends on a more professional preparedness of teachers. Skilled supervisors can help teachers become even more knowledgeable and responsible decision makers.

Some Concluding Thoughts:

If the challenges facing teacher education in Africa in the Twenty-first Century have to be met, then partnership in the educational enterprise must be considered as key in searching for appropriate and lasting solutions to the identified problems. In connection with this, this paper proposes a paradigm where the four major actors (parents, teachers, students and society) must interact and relate to each other. Decisions concerning the governance of teaching and the teaching field must be made jointly by administrators, teachers, parents and students who are the beneficiaries of school programs.

More specifically, the resource centers proposed in this paper especially at the local and National levels should:

(i)   bring together representatives (parents, teachers, university based lecturers, administrators and teacher trainers) for reflection, problem-solving, brain-storming on current and pressing educational issues.

(ii)   develop a deeper understanding of teaching through a more extensive exposure to the school context.

(iii)   encounter different philosophies that teachers hold and to analyze how these inform teaching.

(iv)   realize that changes in the teaching and learning environment are desirable, but that institutional constraints may prevent philosophies and aims from being fully realized in the classroom, at least in the short term.

(v)   develop an awareness of the possibility for change, personal development and know that education can not be an elixir for the many social ills in our society.

At the regional level, it is recommended that ARTRC, establishes an evaluation ad hoc committee that will monitor Teacher Education programs in Africa. The data obtained from such an undertaking can serve as a store of knowledge about innovative programs. Evaluation is an element of socioeconomic research designed to improve methods and approaches to activities relating to social and economic change and development.

In this regard, evaluation efforts will serve as an important basis for regional and national exchange of experience in the development of methodology in teacher education in Africa.

References

Beard, R., & Hauley, D. (1984). Teaching and learning in higher education. London: Harper and Row.

Chapman, R., & Taylor, A. (1970). Principles and practice of education: Teaching training in Africa (2nd ed). London: Collins London and Glasgow Ltd.

Ekane, W. (1992). The use of educational technology: An indispensable option for improving pedagogic practices at the university setting. Association Internationale de Pedagogie Universite's,143-146.

Ekane, W. (1993). "Regional cooperation and higher education." Paper presented at the International Conference in West African Integration. Unpublished manuscript.

Foshay, A. (1967). Professional education: The discipline of the act. Theory into Practice, (6), 224 -230.

Tanner, D., & Tanner, L. N. (1980). Curriculum Development: theory into practice (2nd ed.). New York: Macmillan.

UNECA. (1994). Education staff training development programme. Addis Ababa: ECA .

UNECA. (1994). Reorientation of educational curriculum towards new development challenges and education for peace. Addis Ababa: ECA.

CHAPTER 13

CHALLENGES FOR AFRICAN EDUCATION
IN THE 21st CENTURY

William N. Ekane, Ph.D.
Associate Professor
Department of Teacher Education
College of Education
Grambling State University

Nelson Ngoh, Ph.D.
Lydia Luma, Ph.D.
University of Yaounde I
E.N.S. BP 47, Yaounde
Cameroon

An Overview of the Undesirable of the 20th Century.

A succinct description of the past and present situation of the African was postulated in the introductory comments of the report of the Pan-African conference on Education (1984) on the topic "What school for Africa in the year 2000?" It states:

"The African peoples are currently in a difficult situation. Ignorance,
disease and famine are threatening their very existence, their
sovereignty and their independence. The school of today, inherited
from the colonial period, has not been able to solve these problems.
In many cases, because of its unsuitability, it has even worsened
them. At Kampala, at Niamey as at Yaounde the message has
been clear and specific   the African school must be transformed
so that Africa can effectively take in hand its own destiny and development".

We are in complete agreement with these remarks because we believe that the school system in any locality around the world is the laboratory where individuals can be trained in order to bring about meaningful and authentic change and serve as a human instrument of development. The African school as we perceive it has hitherto not played an effective role in educating the individual to enable him to contribute fully to the overall development of the African society.

An examination and discussion of some pertinent areas that are yet to be desired follows.

School Programs

As indicated earlier, the real problem with school programs is that African teachers everywhere and at all levels are still using outdated curricula which do not take into consideration the actual needs of society.

African Teachers and the Teaching Situation

Worse still is the condition of the African teacher. He is either not being properly trained or not trained at all. Anyone who can talk, scribble on the blackboard or who has connections with the authorities that be, could eventually find himself given the chance to teach in a classroom setting. Yet, as Willard (1964) aptly suggests, we cannot harbor mediocrity among those who presume to provide the inscription our children need for their trying years ahead.

While it could be argued that ethnic/tribal/regional considerations cannot be totally avoided in educational planning, recruitments, or promotions, it is a well known fact that in Africa, the ethnic component is what overrules. Little or no attention is given to merit, competence, output or performance. Furthermore, the twentieth century African teacher appears to have lost track of his mission. He has deserted the very standards, values and ethics that are the raison d'être of his profession. The African teacher has most unfortunately, given in to corruption, materialism and a total lack of professionalism. One thing is clear; teacher morale, prestige and conduct cannot be put on a platter of gold. Neither can these attributes come by decree. They have to be earned by those who merit them.

Teacher Training colleges still follow a curriculum that does not reflect the needs of the modern child in his fast evolving society. Teachers and teacher-trainers themselves have little opportunity available to upgrade their skills in handling children and improving the school curriculum. The result is that these teachers have nothing to offer by way of inspiration to the students. School libraries that are supposed to serve as scholars' gold-mines are ill-equipped with outdated books, reference texts and even lack basic teaching aids, not to mention the new technological tools that are known to enhance the teaching-learning process.

Illiteracy and the African Woman

128

Another important area that deserves consideration is the aspect of illiteracy and the African woman. Studies carried out on education to assess the level of literacy in the continent are dismal at best (Luma, 1983) These studies reveal that 70% of illiterates in Africa are women. Our society has deliberately ignored the fact that basic education begins at home where the woman is naturally the first teacher. The African individual, therefore, is perpetually functionally illiterate because his/her primary source of education (the woman or mother) has not been adequately educated.

African Universities

In Africa as in many other developing countries of the world, schools and universities in particular are looked upon as the source of remedy for their underdevelopment. In the past century, African universities have played this role to an appreciable extent but much is still to be desired.

If African universities have to be much more serviceable to needs of Africans in the 21st century than they are now, there is an urgent need for a change in the structure and organization of our existing universities. The agenda for this change must reflect a national commitment to redesign our educational system that will substantially improve the expectations, aspirations and achievements of an increasing African population. As Busia (1962) observed, "of all Africa's resources, her young people are the most valuable". They are those who will bring about change and development in the 21st century Africa. African universities should therefore be concerned about the quality of the products from these institutions.

Present day African universities have failed and are still failing in their mission to provide adequate education and opportunity for their graduates to develop and apply their skills and aptitudes for the development of the continent. Whereas the African university is supposed to produce the finest minds and products for African development, her curricula do not appear to respond to this need. They are outdated, ineffective, consequently, university graduates cannot find work which matches their skills and knowledge in their society.

Most of the research undertaken by scholars does not look serious. Some of the so-called research findings are either repetitive or unconsumable in the African society itself. We need research on creating effective management techniques that will enable the individual teacher to organize the classroom in such a way that the learner can get a clear picture of what is going on and what is

129

expected of him. The acquisition of effective classroom management techniques will allow teachers to identify successful and unsuccessful strategies in their methods
- repertoire and make appropriate changes. We also need studies to be carried out on how to make our teachers creative, resourceful and competitive and to design self-motivated instruction to utilize revolutionary educational media and modern technology which will help eliminate traditional modes of packaging and delivering instruction in the classroom.

    (a)   Academic Freedom

    The lack of academic freedom or more specifically, university freedom, has been one of those handicaps which have made it impossible for Africans to reap the right fruit from their universities. Many African universities have been politicized and decisions essential to the life of the people are taken by politicians. While stating that a university must not become a pawn for politicians, Ashby (1964) remarked that academic policy must be responsive to legitimate demands from the state. Our universities need to have the academic freedom:
freedom to recruit their staff, admit their students, determine their standards and freedom to design and redesign their curricula. It is when our academicians of the 21st century are free to make maximum use of their own reasonings, without impositions by non-academicians, that our universities can boast of serving the essential needs of the state.

    However, if African universities are going to be powerful instruments for change as in other countries, they must go into partnership with the state. In this case, the university is delegated some powers while the state exerts influence on certain spheres of interests within the university.

    (b)   The University Teacher

    The Pan-African Conference on Education held in Yaounde from 2 - 9th of April 1984 declared that no educational system can rise above the quality of its teachers. This shows the importance of the quality of the teacher for the 21st century. There is need for better qualified teachers in general and a high level of professionalism in particular. Well trained teachers can transform our universities into productive forces in order to develop producers and not only consumers as is the case today. This teacher quality has been confirmed by Coombs (1985) who says that the quality of education and the learning achievement of students depend heavily on the competence, personality, and dedication of the teacher.

Our universities, have to a certain extent, been doing their duty of training graduates for teacher training colleges, secondary schools, and technical institutes. One may wonder why the cry of lack of teachers from the teaching profession to more lucrative professions and careers in the civil service and other public and private agencies. Perhaps, these teachers escape for other jobs because the teaching profession in our century has neither prestige nor the remuneration that other comparable professions and careers command.

(c)   Cooperation Within the University Staff

The African university teacher has been working single-handedly. The sharing of ideas and cooperation are lacking among university teaching staff. This is an undesirable trait. There needs to be team work by teachers within the learning activities and process central to the curriculum. Exchange of ideas among professionals will increase general and individual efficiency.

It has been realized (Tolley, 1990) that the ability to work purposefully with others has always been a basic demand for a satisfying personal life and for achieving a harmonious society. It will be a good thing for the 21st century if this spirit of team teaching is extended to include foreign universities. Profitable cooperation among institutions of higher learning in Africa could be in the domain of sharing materials, and developing facilities for common African use.

(d)   Condition of Work and Morale of Teachers and Students

The quality of education in our universities also depends on the conditions under which the teachers and students are working. For example, like is the case of the university of Yaounde, class sizes are becoming unmanageable. It is not a situation conducive to learning when one teacher has to deliver lectures using microphones to thousands of anxious students cramped in undersized amphitheaters. Others stand stretching their necks to see a diagram or an equation on the chalkboard. These students who are often distant from their lecturers, strain their ears to catch a word of wisdom from the invisible professor. Westerby (1990) recognized that the physical environment in which children learn is a major factor in raising morale and improving motivation. He comments that "drab and shabby" rooms and buildings contribute to "drab and shabby" work and attitudes.

This problem of overcrowding in our universities is aggravated by lack of ample supply of equipment, and other learning materials. Science plays

131

an important role in the development of each country. The number of students in our university science laboratories is so large that very few students usually have access to the limited science apparatus. Our students therefore end up not learning to do science but only learning about science as if science were history learned by listening. By the 21st century, African countries will not be any better developed than they are now if measures are not taken to solve these problems.

Another aspect that needs to be emphasized is that of morale amongst teachers and students. There is no doubt that morale in our universities has deteriorated at an alarming rate and leaves nothing to be desired. There is need for concerted effort on the part of parents, government, community, society. Low morales have been seen to be resulting from failure of heads and senior staff to motivate students because of lack of ability or lack of effort or simply where there is lack of support and encouragement from the higher authorities If we hope to achieve any ideal in the 21st century, morale in education services must be improved for determined, competent and caring leadership amongst our students.

The 21st century is only 6 years away and therefore African educators must hurry to make up for what has been lost either through deliberate action or ignorance in these past centuries. By the 21st century, the ideal would be achieved and the undesirable avoided in the interest of peace if all forces are mobilized towards reducing human suffering in all of its present forms. Africa of the 21st century needs an educational approach that will brighten the continent's expectations, aspirations, knowledge, skills and achievement for a better and more rewarding life. Poverty, unemployment and the rampant spread of diseases should also be checked.

Africa must look for new ways of motivating learners by improving the quality of learning. Teaching must not be entrusted into the hands of non-professionals. Materialism and other vices should not be allowed to dominate the minds and aspirations of the children.

To achieve these lofty goals mentioned above, the following is an outline of a plan of action:

1.   Goals, aims, objectives and purposes of all of education, no matter the level, must be clearly defined and the steps of implementation properly delineated, taking into consideration the realities, and as-aspirations of our society. Qualified teachers and other educationists should be involved in this exercise

132

2. We should quickly come to grips with the fact that we are in an era of consultation and dialogue, where the team-teaching approach is far superior to our traditional individualism in teaching and transmission. In other words, we are advocating for a collectivist spirit of solving our problems. This will create an atmosphere or forum for concertation, dialogue, and free exchange of ideas. The African teacher has worked so hard and so long in isolation and competition, and we believe time has come for a real cooperative and collaborative effort in solving our common problems. We propose team-teaching within subject areas as a viable option.

3. We propose that we must not only learn how to use the new technologies but study ways of how to produce these technologies. This means that we must teach our young how to build up computers and be able to repair them when they are defunct. Erundrett (1990) however warns that the use of microcomputers in schools does not itself guarantee the existence of a satisfactory educational curriculum. Africa must return to the basics even in the methods of teaching sciences and the languages as well as in the methods of discharging their daily activities.

4. Moral education must be included in our primary, secondary and tertiary educational curricula because through it the principles of peace, the respect of other human beings and upholding the dignity of mankind will be fostered.

5. The African woman should have her rightful place in our society. Statistics on the state of the woman are revealing : women have only 4 places out of 100 places in ministerial or decision making positions in the world. In Africa, a meager 2.5% of decision-making positions is reserved for women whereas 97.5% is monopolized by men (UN, 1989). Furthermore, if female peasants could be educated, our society as a whole would do better economically and socially. African women should be given the opportunity to study and be encouraged to aspire to positions of leadership. After all women already have given mankind able leadership elsewhere - Indira Gandhi, Butho, Thatcher and Corazino are glaring examples. The terms of office of these ladies should not be considered as an end in themselves but rather as an

indication of the pattern that the 21st century should look like for Africa and the world as a whole.

6. Adapting innovative means that deal with the problems of ignorance, disease, the handicapped, unemployment, and ways being humane to others should be included in our educational programs. In addition, teachers of 21st century Africa must arm themselves with skills and knowledge that will enable them

-to dispense education in such a way that it allows for every African child to integrate themselves fully and functionally as productive members of their respective societies.

-to give opportunity for African individuals to be creative and ingenious so that only the sky can serve as the limit to their aspirations.

7. The curriculum of the 21st century must at all levels of education be

-adapted to national realities or societal needs.

-adapted to open up channels of dialogue and cooperation.

-designed to pursue excellence in order to eliminate ignorance and illiteracy.

-designed to promote culture that makes an individual to become self-reliant and self-propagating in his society.

8. Teachers should be given special training on how to improvise teaching and learning materials and how to cause students to get involved in active learning themselves. University authorities should tighten the university admission requirements. This is in a bid to reduce intake in order to admit only high quality students since university education is not meant for mediocres. The practice of paying students to learn should be stopped. Students should be made to pay fees in order to receive the available university teaching and learning opportunities.

9. Our teacher training programs must aim "at raising the best men and women that can be got for the purpose of educating, controlling and directing our children and youth, who will eventually become the nucleus of our future generations. Good teacher training is the best and only way to ensure that every African child is given the best education of which he is capable, by

the best African teacher possible. Only through serious realistic, and dedicated teacher education can each respective African government and country properly and adequately educate each of its citizens to the extent where each can achieve personal excellence and render the best possible service to his African society and the world at large..." (Luma, 1983, p.9).

10.   In the 21st century, emphasis should be put on the utilitarian functions of African universities. Deliberate efforts should be made to incorporate into undergraduate courses elements of indigenous African civilization.

In conclusion, we wish to reiterate that the real challenge for the African school in the 21st century is adopting innovative, creative and imaginative strategies of transforming our educational institutions into functioning units that will better serve the African individual and society. That is, African schools must, in the 21st century, not only sincerely seek to preserve their present loyalty to the western tradition; they must also discover and proclaim a loyalty to progressive indigenous values of the African culture and society.

References

Ashby, E., & Busia, K. A. (1962). The functions of West African universities in the West African intellectual community. Nigeria: Ibadan University Press.

Ashby, E. (1964). African universities and western tradition. London: Oxford University Press.

Brundrett, M. (1990, September). Information technology across the curriculum: A radical approach to implementation. Journal of the College of Preceptors, 40(30).

Coombs, P. H. (1985). The world crisis in education. New York: Oxford University Press.

Luma, L. E. (1993). The education of African teachers. Yaounde: SOPECAM.

Pan-African Conference in Education (1984). What school for Africa in the year 2000. Yaounde: UN Dept. of Public Information.

Westerby, R. K. (1990). Sir Philip Magnus Memorial Lecture "The challenge of the 1990s: Education Today".

Tolley, G. (1990). Challenges for education. London: Education Journal of College of Preceptors .

Willard, A. (1964). A time for teaching. New York: Harper & Row.

CHAPTER 14

REGIONAL COOPERATION AND HIGHER EDUCATION

William N. Ekane, Ph.D.
Associate Professor
Department of Teacher Education
College of Education
Grambling State University
Grambling, LA

INTRODUCTION

The aforementioned problems pose significant and compelling demands on higher education in general and those of the West African educational systems in particular. We envisage many of these problems being solved through regional cooperation and integration in university institutions whose prime mission should be to develop and apply the skills and aptitudes of graduates for the development of the West African states and perhaps Africa as a whole.

WHY COOPERATE?

There are glaring and compelling reasons why to be advanced institutions of higher learning need to cooperation-operate in the West African region. First, the limitation of human and material potentials in some of the West African states and the crying need for governments to raise skilled manpower in the various academic disciplines to meet the needs of the respective nations calls for inter-university Cooperation. Also, university institutions are extremely expensive to establish and maintain. There must be adequate provision for such institutions because they require well equipped libraries, laboratories, book shops as well as a Printing Press.

Second, the West African scholars and university teachers have by and large lived and worked in isolation from their colleagues and counterparts for too long (Beard et al, 1984). The lack of contact and communication with one another has left many scholars guessing what might be going on in other campuses. They need to know specific information about relevant merits and intensive work being done in their disciplines. Open lines of communication with one another as well as with scholars from the outside world are vital to the success of their work and scholarship.

Furthermore, the contemporary teacher faces the difficult task of developing students to handle the diverse changing and challenging needs of the community through programs that emphasize the integration of theory with practice. In addition, the university lecturer does not only have the arduous task of designing and implementing new delivery strategies using state-of-the-art technologies to accommodate large classes but also needs to design a value-oriented education suited for complete human development and responsible citizenship in our contemporary society (Ekane, 1992). In sum, the students ought to be taught to work in different conditions from those they were trained, think productively, read intelligently and exercise proficiency in their respective areas of specialization.

Third, cooperation is an index of civilization. Man has the fundamental urge to interact with others and also to adapt himself to his environment. Therefore, a pooling of human resources and experiences would surely be of great value in a West African inter-university cooperation.

This chapter does not only advocate closer cooperation among institutions of higher learning in the several territories in West Africa but has as its ultimate objective that this cooperation bring about a deepening of understanding between the governments and people in this region and thus help to foster the realization of genuine integration. Since the West African region faces common or similar problems, cooperation efforts should be encouraged in the areas of science and technology, engineering, economics, business management, commerce, medicine, agriculture and other disciplines in order that we can make immediate and practical contributions to development.

Before we discuss concrete and possible areas of inter-regional or inter-university cooperation, there are some common problems that have to be overcome if meaningful and fruitful collaborative efforts must take place. Some of the major problems which readily come to mind are political, linguistic, and financial.

POLITICAL

In the political domain, every sovereign state has its needs, social priorities as well as growth structures. Each has its policies and pre-planned programs as to how to improve the educational system, provide adequate schooling, master life situations and prepare its youths for employment in agriculture, industry, public and private sectors and in rural and urban centers. For effective collaboration to be

138

undertaken, these issues must never be undermined or ignored. Moreso, the case for according the higher priority to West African cooperation in research is overwhelming, especially research into the cultures of the West African peoples. There is an urgent call for cultural research in order to make the new as well as the old universities truly African. Such fundamental research has to be undertaken into the traditional history, languages and the arts and unless there is collaboration in these areas, the progress will be slow.

LINGUISTIC

From a linguistic perspective, the West African states have two distinct university systems built upon the English and French models. Structurally, the English-speaking universities are private autonomous corporations independent of the state whereas those in the French-speaking zone are attached to a centralized state system. More importantly, the languages used for dispensing instruction are different, thus creating a real barrier in getting information across. Consequently there is a dearth of knowledge about development, and kind of research that is going on and/or that has taken place on either side of the language divide. For example, the French-speaking university of Dakar, the University College of Abidjan, and the University of Lovanuim in the Congo are separated from the English-speaking ones in Sierra Leone, Liberia, Ghana and Nigeria. Because these institutions of higher learning share common problems which cut across linguistic lines in West Africa, it will require the collaboration of persons trained in the two university systems. We also propose that intensified studies in French be carried out in the English speaking universities and the teaching of English be intensified in the French speaking universities.

It must be said that the communication blockage is extant, not only between the two lingua-cultural entities, but indeed within the entities themselves; which is why we would further recommend the establishment of a reasonable network of information flow and exchange among all institutions of higher learning in West Africa through "ARCHE" (the function and meaning of ARCHE will be described later in this chapter).

FINANCIAL

Many well conceived and articulated projects in the African states are not implemented for lack of funding. In order to establish effective collaboration among universities of West Africa we need funding. Such funding can be obtained from a couple of institution--governments, non-governmental organizations and private individual donors in West Africa, and overseas. The real task is identifying foundations and other financial organizations

abroad with special interest in West Africa's educational concerns. The largest and best known are: Ford, Rockefeller, Carnegie, Mission bodies, the Canadian government, U.S. Business firms, UNESCO and best of all the American government which is usually the biggest donor. If these projects are well articulated and submitted to some of the above sources, the chances of securing grants are high.

With the above three key problem areas taken care of, we proceed to identify five possible areas of cooperation among institutions of higher education. They are:

1.   curriculum development
2.   production of resourceful graduates
3.   establishing and maintaining a strong technological network.
4.   staff development and
5.   cultural awareness.

To ensure the effective functioning of the areas identified above, this chapter calls for the creation of an organization called ARCHE which stands for Africa Regional Commission for Higher Education. Under the aegis of ARCHE the following broad goals could be pursued.

A)   Setting the structures of ARCHE
B)   Co-ordinating the functioning of the areas of cooperation outlined above.

Under (A) above we suggest that a governing board and its secretariat be created immediately after the international conference on West Africa Integration. This governing body could constitute, one member from Higher Education designated by each government of the West African states, the vice-chancellor of each West African University or University College and a member nominated or elected by each University Senate of these institutions.

In this way both the political agenda of governments and academic interest of training skilled manpower would be represented on the board. This body should create sub-commissions such as an inter-African council for study and research in higher education that will hasten the adaptation of the West African universities to the cultural, economic and social realities of member countries, enable intellectuals to take a more influential and more constructive place in the

140

shaping of West-African public opinions and development, and improve the quality of intellectual life in West Africa. Furthermore, this sub-commission could stimulate and improve intellectual life through the formation of intellectual communities such as; Association for Social-Anthropology and Sociology, a West African Historical Association, a West African Archeological Association, a West African Museologist Association, a West African Accreditation Association and so on. Once these associations are underway they could become completely independent of the secretariat of the Board. The Board could also create other sub-commissions whenever the need arises to address a particular problem.

Another major function which might be performed by the proposed inter-university Board is the creation of a clearing-house for current research on West Africa problems conducted in West Africa and abroad in all the various fields in which institutions of higher education are concerned (i.e., agriculture, animal breeding, African History, African Arts etc.); the establishment of a West African University press for publication of scientific and scholarly work on problems of West African interest; the development of methods of instruction in English and French in elementary, secondary and university levels; the pooling of knowledge about university building and maintenance problems; the establishment of a region-wide survey of supply and demand for highly educated personnel in all disciplines and the pooling of knowledge and effective strategies on how to deal with the acute problems such as disproportionate teacher/student ratio just to mention these (Workshop on distant learning, 1987).

Funding for ARCHE to start work could easily be obtained by first identifying and clearly articulating the need and goals of the Board and presenting them in a more unified and co-ordinated way to local governments and foreign organizations (like UNESCO or the U.S. government that are interested in West African educational problems). With the establishment of ARCHE an ad hoc committee could be assigned to work out the constitution, criteria for membership, type of organization and administration, and present needs in a forceful comprehensive and interesting way to foreign organizations interested in supporting higher education in West Africa. A further short term goal of ARCHE could be to set up another ad hoc committee that will gather information on all West Africa universities--their programs and structures so as to come up with a handbook on West Africa Institutions of higher education. Members of the ad hoc committee must be distinguished scholars versed in English and French. This and other ad hoc committees must report to the governing body of ARCHE.

141

The work of this latter ad hoc committee could conceivably provide data and facts about what is available and what is happening in these respective universities. For example, it will highlight pertinent information about their programs of study, their curricula, their staff problems and so forth. This handbook would spark initiatives about doing something on the university programs. In this wise, cooperation will happen as a natural course of events and the consequences of such inquiry will hopefully stimulate such question as what is going to be the place of governments and what part are the institutions of higher education going to play in this scheme.

Out of the work of the ad hoc committees could emerge collaboration in (B) above, and the areas that were mentioned earlier are curriculum development; production of resources graduates; establishing and maintaining a strong technological network; staff development and cultural awareness. Let us examine each of these aspects in turn.

Curriculum Development

With an inherited and transported model of university education from France for the French universities and by Britain for the English oriented universities, much is still to be desired of the kind of knowledge, skills and attitudes transmitted because they meet the needs neither of the learner nor society. Africa needs curricula that are adapted to the learners' needs and aspirations and oriented towards the reality of the African culture.

For example, a majority of the textbooks used especially at university level are authored and printed abroad (Berghe, 1973; Yoloye, 1986). One cannot talk of making curriculum and content appropriate to meet West African needs while we are still using foreign textbooks. There is therefore perhaps a genuine obligation to write textbooks which will be the core of the African arts and sciences curricula. More importantly, in an attempt to adapt university studies in the West African context, we must put African studies at the core of the curriculum especially at the undergraduate level. A great deal of research has still to be done in the African studies curriculum--that is in history, society, language, economy, political institutions, ecology, as well as values, cosmology, and philosophy. It is a task which requires inter-disciplinary as well as inter-university cooperation. A further area for cooperation is the building of a structure which will necessitate closer approximation of syllabi, length of university terms, mode and standards of examination and qualification and recruitment of teaching staff.

142

The information obtained from closer approximation of programs and structures will enhance the work of the Accreditation board that was earlier proposed. The Accreditation board under the auspices of ARCHE will co-ordinate the validation of degree courses in member universities, the transfer of credit hours by students who want to study in other institutions and empower the use of Pidgin English by giving it official status as a lingua franca for the West African states.

Another possible area of fruitful inter-university cooperation might exist in combining knowledge and experience built up on subjects of specifically African interest where both French and English university systems can offer a very substantial contribution. These courses should be tailored to suit the needs of the West African society and ought to begin at the primary and secondary levels where subjects such as history, geography, civics, natural sciences need to be taught against the background of the African culture. We will now discuss the products from existing university systems.

Producing Resourceful Graduates

Many graduates who are products of the West African universities have acquired knowledge and skills that are ill-suited for the demands of their respective societies. This mismatch of supply of trained graduates on the one hand and the demand for skilled manpower on the other hand has brought about high rates of massive unemployment. Again this unemployment situation could be blamed on our extant West African university curricula. One way of redressing this situation as stated earlier is by designing curricula that might meet the needs and aspiration of the African culture. A second path to tackling this problem is the exchange of scholars, both at the undergraduate and graduate levels.

In order for this to happen, all West African universities concerned must aim at standards which are comparable. The publication of the handbook on West Africa institutions of higher learning, will provide valuable information that will eventually lead to harmonized entry standard for students and recruitment of teaching staff, the length of courses offered and more importantly their content. It is envisaged that through inter-university cooperation we get to know and understand one other better. This will promote an authentic integration of West Africa states. A third approach to resolving this problem of producing resourceful graduates is carrying out research based on local needs. Since societies' demands are not currently being met by our graduates, a large scale study could jointly be undertaken by the respective institutions in order to identify the short, medium

143

and long term goals of our societies. More concretely, research could be carried out with the purpose of bringing about a massive breakthrough in serving the continent of Africa and contributing to scholarship and learning in the domain of local herbs, medicinal plants and barks of trees, rediscovering the potentialities of traditional doctors and studying their profession to make it more scientific. Other areas of possible research could be focused on; agriculture, trade, communication, and the African chiefdoms, just to mention these.

A fourth strategy could be pursued through the formation of West African professional and cultural bodies. In this way regional co-operation can be actively fostered. For example, lawyers, agriculturists, writers, teachers, engineers could organize themselves into professional associations and meet regularly to discuss concerns common to their professions. This will be useful in that various universities could work together and share knowledge and experiences to improve their professions and the young prospective graduates will through conferences, gain valuable insights as to what is expected of them when they go into the labor market.

True and authentic integration cannot take place within the West African states without creating a free labor market for the region. To achieve this goal, the joint efforts of the institutions of higher education should aim at producing graduates who will have versatile knowledge and skills, capable of working in different conditions from those they are trained in. The graduates ought to be able to think productively, communicate fluently and develop thorough insight into personal relationship. Finally, West African universities could jointly carry out research on refresher courses to give graduates the skills that will best serve their respective societies. ARCHE will be called upon here to establish an institute where university graduates could be recycled so that they are useful and functional in the West African communities. Such an institution would offer training in specialized disciplines so that the West African community would benefit from the services of skilled manpower adapted to their needs. During the course of study, the graduates will learn to adapt to new techniques in their learning patterns, study how to obtain information, and know how to apply it in new and varying situations. These and other more demanding requirements for students in our changing and challenging society point to a reorientation of higher education. We shall now turn to the third area where collaboration among West African states is crucial.

144

Establishing and maintaining a strong technological network

Communication between scholars across national boundaries is not only an essential for the advancement of knowledge but one of the most hopeful means of advancing international and regional harmony.

The dearth of information flow and exchange is very evident among the African universities in general and those of the West African institutions of higher education in particular. Social and technological changes affect the patterns of university provision and ways of teaching and learning. Therefore, since there is no network where books, articles, professional journals and other useful pedagogic and instructional materials can be borrowed, or stored, it is difficult to know what is going on elsewhere or even how to obtain new information and how to share new findings from research with colleagues in same or other disciplines. At the level of ARCHE, we proposed the creation of a Clearing House and Library. The Library will be something similar to the Library of Congress in the USA. This newly created library can operate exchanges of publications and experiments with inter-university borrowing of documents and rare books. Such a library could serve as an effective sphere for cooperation in micro-filming of files, of newspapers, periodicals and journals which are absolutely essential. This endeavor will attract staff capable of doing the kind of research required. The scholars working on this project could jointly work with universities where there are institutes of African studies with reasonably good libraries. These microfilms could be useful to American, Canadian, and British universities and others, many of which want to build up source materials in African studies and are reluctant to spend so much in trying to get files, newspaper and scientific journals.

The clearinghouse could also prepare an annotated inventory of completed, continuing and projected research endeavors in all institutions of West Africa. Until such a time as both English and French are easily interchangeable languages for West Africa intellectuals, it will also serve to overcome the language barrier by producing its inventory in both French and English indicating the original language of the work at all times. The clearing house could as well carry out research on the proposed lingua franca of the West African states--which is Pidgin English with the aim of upgrading it to official status like English and French. Such a clearing house could equally serve those who are grappling with evaluating the priorities of research projects and also serve as a guide in making fellowship awards, and for those who are undertaking research work.

145

The proposed inter-university clearing house could further serve to provide bibliographical material on crucial subjects like economics, agriculture, anthropology, business and languages, just to mention these. Information could be supplied to the clearing house by member institutions in the region, and other interested bodies. The use of computer automation will facilitate these tasks. Computer centers in each institution need to set up modems and phone lines and these could all be hooked up with the clearing house located at the Headquarters--which will be decided upon by the governing body of ARCHE.

Another major area to be explored by West Africa institutions of higher education to overcome the poor communication flow is through the use of mass-media, television, radio and machine-programmed teaching in transmitting knowledge, skills and attitudes and even brainstorming on common problems affecting the West African communities. ARCHE could co-ordinate the work of university departments of education or institutes of education to direct their attention, investigation, deliberately seeking and experimenting with new processes, not only in actual instruction, in content, in organization, but in the very media that they are using. This again demands inter-university cooperation to be successful and hopefully will enhance regional integration.

Since we have common educational and economic problems in West Africa, it could be a good idea to debate some of these issues openly, through Teleconferencing from time to time. Teleconferencing is a powerful medium that brings countries and peoples closer and almost face to face. One gets not only to hear but also to see the speaker as he/she appears on the screen. In Cameroon, we watch a U.S. based Telecast of "African Journal and WorldNet", transmitted live from Washington by satellite where Africans from different countries ask Americans experts questions pertaining to the American political life. This medium could be an excellent way to exchange views our common problems.

Finally, the range of knowledge these days is enormous and no new or existing institutions can single-handedly provide facilities for covering all disciplines. Therefore, this chapter purposes inter-university co-operation in at least two domains:

(1)   Sharing teaching facilities.

The poorer West African countries who cannot own or run a university could send their students to a sister African institution of higher education instead of sending them abroad. It is a lot cheaper to do so. Also, for the existing universities each should be free to establish faculties and department as it deems necessary, but in planning these teaching facilities all the universities should co-operate. For example, after establishing some basic faculties such as Arts and Sciences, universities could try to specialize (as some are doing) in faculties for which they are best suited. Would it not be wise for students from Cameroon and other states to study in Darkar's Pharmacology school instead of developing theirs? Would it not also be wise for West African states to develop fully the medical school in Ibadan, economics in Accra, engineering in Kumasi, archeology in IFE and translation in Cameroon since structures are already in place, thereby creating a free flow of eligible students into these institutions instead of each country trying to develop its own? These facilities for common African or West Africa use could enhance regional and continental integration.

(2)   Research institutions

Inter-West African co-operation seems even more feasible in the research domain. Research could be conducted in cocoa, rubber, coffee, cattle and so forth. Should each university aim at providing a full complement of faculties then arrangements could be made for interchange of staff and students. Let us now discuss ways of fostering co-operation of existing staff.

STAFF DEVELOPMENT

Due to the lack of communication flow and exchange of ideas among staff in the West African institutions of higher learning, there is an intellectual slum. The primary functions of the faculty at the university are teaching and research. All staff need to improve upon their teaching techniques and keep abreast with current research, without which a university teacher becomes unproductive. This chapter therefore proposes regional co-operation in .higher education among its staff in order to promote academic excellence in member institutions.

In this case, ARCHE should organize seminars and colloquia on a regular and rotatory basis with expert addressing varying subject matters, to allow participants from other countries to benefit at their point of felt need. Some of the participatory approaches could be designed to influence need assessments, course planning, content, methods, familiarization of the state-of-the-art in the novel technologies such computers and their assessors and evaluation techniques. As a consequence such personnel exchanges could enhance co-operation and the likelihood of a real exchange of thought and discussion may take place. These short term staff development courses could improve the teaching performances of

147

faculty and hopefully foster behavioral patterns that are capable of developing critical attitude of mind, objectivity and discursive reflection on given problems.

This chapter further proposes that faculty members take study tours to other institutions in West Africa and these tours could be co-ordinated by ARCHE and/or directly with the host institutions. The benefits from such study tours are great if they are well planned.

Institutions that want to organize workshops or seminars could also call upon ARCHE to assist them at a local level. This kind of open opportunity for nationals to share their expertise with other experts may develop their own capacity to become trainers of trainers. This brings us to our fifth and final area of possible inter-university collaboration.

CULTURAL AWARENESS

There is no doubt that West African states are rich in cultural diversity. Little has been done to exploit our varying and diverse cultural heritage to benefit the West African community and continent. Again we encourage ARCHE to co-ordinate this activity by creating a West Africa Regional Museum of Arts. Each West African country may be asked to donate works of arts, crafts, paintings etc. This great museum would generate revenue from tourists and other interested persons.

Another way of promoting cultural awareness is by organizing every two years, an inter-territorial festival of African arts and literature. This festival could be held on a rotatory basis. Other African countries could be invited to attend. On display could be such activities as traditional African dances, music, works of arts; such as handicrafts, metal and leather works, wood carvings, ceramics, and works of literature such as; poems, short plays, as well as marketing products. It is probable that the results of such inter-territorial festivals is likely to bring closer union between the states and foster a higher standard of performance and cultural awareness and diversity.

Schools of higher education should also be encouraged to design and produce programs that seek to develop morally responsible individuals who could combine career competence with cultural awareness and intellectual curiosity. In addition, West African universities should be encouraged to develop courses in group dynamics that will enable students to study our diverse and rich culture and be able to lead discussions, accept points of views different from theirs and contribute effectively to discussions on the African culture.

CONCLUSION

In order to co-ordinate and enhance regional integration in the West African states in general and the inter-university collaboration in particular, this chapter recommends the creation of an organization called ARCHE. The mission of ARCHE could, perhaps, be best spelt out in its constitution, being made up of the following defined functions. It should

- promote dialogue, particularly with respect to the exchange of information on higher education among member institutions, and others with regard its modus of operation, its priority areas and the experiences expected;

- assist member countries to create national centers for curriculum development where   they do not exist and strengthen existing ones in order to bring African studies into the core of humanistic studies;

- create ways to raise funds from member countries and especially from donor organizations to finance projects;

- establish an accreditation board to validate degree programs in universities of member countries;

- empower the use of Pidgin English and give it official status as the lingua franca for the West African region;

- serve as a clearing house to store and disseminate innovation in the area of education and technology;

- provide information on programs, strategies, currently available pools of knowledge and means to plan feasible strategies for the future;

- set up an educational network, institutionalized and manpower development plans;

- establish a library that will serve for inter-university borrowing of resource materials;

- offer a series of scholarship programs and short term training courses, study tours, personal exchange programs and cultural extravaganzas among member universities and states.

In sum, the novel ideas and strategies advanced in this chapter on inter-university co-operation have great potential in enhancing not only the quality and quantity of programs of member institutions but are likely to meet the manpower needs, foster bilateral and multilateral co-operation

149

among member states as well as serve the aspirations of the respective states in the region.

References

Beard, R., & Hartley, D. (1984). Teaching and learning in higher education. London: Harper & Row.

Berghe, P. (1973). Power and privilege at an African university. London: Routledge and Kegan Paul.

Ekane, W. (1992). The use of educational technology : An indispensable option for improving pedagogic practices at the university setting. Paper accepted for publication in the Association Internationale de Pedagogie Universite.

Yoloye, E. (1986). Achievement, problems and prospects. Curriculum Development Programs in Africa. German Foundation for International Development (DSE).

Workshop on distant learning. (1987). Advanced communication technologies in education. University of Yaounde Chancellery.

CHAPTER 15

TEACHING AIDS AND THEIR EFFECTS ON ACADEMIC PERFORMANCE: A CASE STUDY OF FOUR SELECTED ANGLOPHONE PRIMARY SCHOOLS IN YAOUNDE

William N. Ekane, Ph.D.
Associate Professor
Department of Teacher Education
College of Education
Grambling State University
Grambling, LA

M. A. Mbangwana, Ph.D.
B. Matchinda, Ph.D.
Ecole Normale Superieure
Yaounde, Cameroon

ABSTRACT

The purpose of this study was to find out how often primary school teachers use teaching aids, of whatever type, in the course of teaching. It was also aimed at finding out the effects of using teaching aids on the pupils' academic performance. The study was delimited only to Anglophone teachers and pupils of primary schools in Yaounde. The survey research design was used to carry out the research. By this design, the questionnaire for teachers and experimentation pre-test and post-test) on class six pupils were the instruments used to collect data for the study.

A simple random sampling technique was used to select four Anglophone primary schools in Yaounde. The same sampling technique was used to select the class six pupils that were experimented upon. All the teachers of the four schools were administered questionnaires. Out of the sixty eight teachers that were used in the study, forty two of them said they use visual aids in the course of teaching. This gave a total percentage of 61.8 %

INTRODUCTION

It is a good policy for the teacher to use as fully as possible the resources that are available in the classroom. This requires that the teacher uses different types of teaching aids in the course of teaching. This is because imagery can easily be developed in the children when teachers present their lessons with demonstrations and illustrations. There exists a wide variety of teaching aids in primary schools which range from simple objects, visuals and audio visual aids such as photographs, flash cards, maps, wallsheets, specimens, radio, television and many others. The choice of the medium to used by the teacher may be influenced by its availability, its convenience in use and its effectiveness.

This piece of work therefore sets out to encourage primary school teachers and pupils to make better use of teaching aids at their disposal in the course of teaching and learning.

STATEMENT OF THE PROBLEM

Many teachers, due to insufficient practical training, do not recognize the importance of teaching materials that are available in the vicinity. Even when such aids are given them, they often find it difficult to use them in full.

Some teachers prefer to use sophisticated audio visual aids to traditional media but they are often scared. This is because as Farrant (1980, p. 334) states:

> *The complexity of some audio visual aids tends to frighten teachers who have had no practical training in its application so that much equipment supplied to schools is grossly under-used.*

In the same light, most teachers, instead of understanding that teaching aids are for making teaching more effective have the idea that they make the teacher's life easier. Consequently they tend to give up as soon as they find what hard work it is making them and planning their use.

RESEARCH QUESTIONS

This study will address the following research questions:

1: How often do primary school teachers use teaching aids in the course of teaching.

2: What are the effects of frequently using teaching aids on children's academic performance in such schools?

SIGNIFICANCE OF THE STUDY

In carrying out this study, we hoped that it will inspire teachers and pupils to adopt the use of teaching aids in the teaching/learning process. The study will also be significant to parents, curriculum planners and the government.

The cognitive development of primary school pupils is still very low and open to maneuver. It will be good for teachers to help these pupils by using every available teaching aid to enhance their observational and analytical abilities. Moreover, this research work was carried out with the hope and aspiration that it will help teachers, pupils and even parents to develop the habit of creativity and invent or produce local teaching aids and also to develop the habit of using modem technological teaching aids like television, video, film and radio.

Student teachers in teacher training institutions, especially those undergoing primary school teacher training, will also benefit from this study. It will make them realize the importance and necessity of teaching aids and thus enable them to adopt their use in the course of teaching. This will make them better exploit the teaching aids that are available in schools where they have been posted. This piece of work will also be significant to the government as it will enable her enforce the use of teaching aids in primary schools by enacting legislation requiring to assess how often primary school teachers use teaching aids. This will be supervised by the Ministry of National Education.

Finally this study will be of significance to curriculum planners in the sense that they may institute new subject areas in the curriculum that will require extensive and frequent use of teaching aids as this will enhance the teaching/learning process.

RESEARCH HYPOTHESES

Ha1: Pupils who are frequently taught using simple objects and other visual aids will perform significantly better than those who are taught without them.

Ha2: Pupils whose teachers frequently use audio aids in the course of teaching will perform significantly better than those who are taught without such aids.

SCOPE OF THE STUDY

155

The study was limited only to Anglophone primary schools within Yaounde, in the center province of Cameroon. The study also limited itself to primary school teachers and the class pupils of such schools. Class six pupils were chosen because there we expected them to have a sound knowledge about teaching aids.

The study did not deal only with studying the effects of locally produced teaching aids on pupils' performance but it extended to those teaching aids which are electrically operated

REVIEW OF RELATED LITERATURE

Teaching aids cover different forms of symbol systems (sounds, moving pictures, charts, maps etc.) and each has its own potential in terms of the teaching or learning that it can effectively promote. Most teaching aids are flexible, in that each can be used for a variety of teaching functions. However, while most teaching aids can present abstract knowledge and ideas, which are mainly conveyed through the use of spoken or written language, some of them are able to present concrete examples of objects, processes and events.

For the purpose of convenience, this section will be divided into three subsections according to the broad classification of teaching aids which are; visual aids, audio visual aids and audio aids.

VISUAL AIDS

Teaching aids that fall under this category include, among others, the blackboard, real objects (specimens), charts, posters, maps and globes. The blackboard is a teaching aid par excellence in primary schools. Many authors have attributed other names to it, such as Mugglestone (1980, p. 33) who states:

> The blackboard is also called the chalkboard because
> it takes on a variety of colors.

The blackboard is one of the traditional tools of the teacher and remains an important teaching aid today in most technologically sophisticated classrooms. Gower and Steve (1983, p. 159) affirm this by stating that:

> The chalkboard is the most useful and most common
> teaching aid that any classroom must possess. It serves
> as a visual testimony of the teacher's work and is used

for drawing sketch maps and other simple drawings that
facilitate children's learning.

The obvious advantages of the blackboard are that it is reliable, cheap, always ready for use, simple to use and it has a long life. It has the greatest flexibility and utility. It is widely used in our schools. Okorie (1979, p. 142) quoting Monroe in the Encyclopedia of Education writes:

Blackboards have become so much a factor in our methods
of work that we really wonder how old time teachers did
without them. They are not only valuable aid in our methods
of presenting many subjects, they serve as a socializing agent
of no small moment. They bring the individual pupil and his
work directly before the whole class, stimulate him to self
dependence and furnish a splendid opportunity for the democratic
give-and-take criticism which he must meet in real life.

REAL OBJECTS, MODELS AND PICTURES

The use of real objects or simple objects (specimens and models) and pictures in teaching helps to make learning natural and enjoyable. Real objects include among others, life plants and animals, tools, weapons. Richard (1966) holds the view that most conventional primary schools should make considerable use of teaching materials such as real or simple objects and models. However, they failed to bring out the effects of using such teaching aids on the pupils performance.

Models and specimens used in the classroom should be big enough to be seen by all the pupils. They must be unambiguous and presentable because they create a need for new language, elicit already known language, supply context for activity and stimulate discussion. They arouse imaginative understanding and appreciation. The teacher evokes in the mind of the pupils images and thought processes. Luma (1983) holds the view that imagery helps the children to understand and remember better.

Pictures are of great value m enhancing the teaching/learning process. Most teachers underestimate the contributions that pictures make to learning. They can be used for direct learning/teaching, tutoring or simply providing some variety in the materials being studied.

Many countries look more closely to basic resources such as pictures and other visuals because electrically-operated teaching aids are expensive. For this reason many teachers now prefer to create their own pictorial materials because they are economical and secondly, teaching that involves visual presentation is more effective than lecturing. Teaching that involves pictures is more superior to lecturing with respect to the amount the pupils remember, the depth of understanding that results and the enjoyment experienced.

CHARTS, MAPS, POSTERS AND FLASH CARDS

Charts are systematic arrangements of facts and relationships in a graphic, pictorial or diagrammatic form. Charts are large sheets of papers, carrying prepared textual and/or graphic and/or pictorial information. They can either be used to display information during the course of a lesson or can be pinned to the walls of a classroom in order to be studied by the pupils in their own time. Mills (1979:192) states that:

Charts displayed in the classroom should be changed regularly
or interest will wane. A wall chart for permanent display may be
an attempt to summarize a whole lesson or a course, and contain
a great deal of explanation. Charts for use in formal instruction
should be simple, clear, easily seen by the class and have only
main points.

Posters, as teaching aids, illustrate a limited form of information. In teaching they may be used to present single action or objects. They may also be part of a sequence of a picture.

Flash cards are also valuable teaching aids that can be used in the classroom. Mostly used to introduce a lesson, flash cards printed with words and/or pictures which can be handled easily by the teacher.

AUDIO/VISUAL AIDS

These are teaching aids that fall under the class in which audio and visual materials are combined to form an integrated instructional system. They include a number of media that are particularly used in collective and individualized instruction. Audio visual equipment facilitate learning since they, in some sense, duplicate the teacher. The value increases when teachers record programs and use them as part of teaching and learning program instead of being bound by the times

158

of broadcast. In order to make children learn better, the teacher should present aids as television, video and film programs or even local materials into the classroom.

Stones (1966, p. 246) refers to these audio visual aids as teaching machines when he states that:

> *Teaching machines available in school are electrical*
> *devices such as film projectors, video and television.*
> *These machines help to motivate younger children since*
> *they derive satisfaction when using them.*

Teaching machines include, among others, video, television, films, slides and computers.

TELEVISION

Television has recently become of popular use in most schools especially those found in urban areas and is mostly used in subject areas like science, social science and language arts and/or reading. Television presents a great deal of information. Barrie and Jill (1980, p. 81) affirm this view when they state that:

> *Not only does learning from television consist of*
> *improving one's knowledge of what is going on*
> *in the world, television is also a major source of*
> *social learning... children then may turn to television*
> *as a source of various kinds of learning. Through*
> *television children may learn about life, about*
> *themselves, about how to behave in different situations,*
> *about how to deal with personal problems etc.*

In Cameroon most children watch television during their leisure time especially when their favorite programs are being broadcasted. They consider television as a source of entertainment and not as a source of learning. However, the Cameroon Radio Television Corporation (CRTV) usually broadcasts such programs as "the usually broadcasts such as 'the debate' and 'thinking time' " over the television which can enrich and improve upon the children's knowledge. Teaching with the use of television will help in providing a source of stimulus for talking, reading and writing.

Despite the educational role that television plays, its use is being neglected because of some obvious reasons. Curriculum planners pay little attention to television as a medium. Television programs are not normally transmitted at convenient times. Many primary schools are not supplied with electricity.

VIDEO

The video is one of the electrically-operated teaching aids which hold a great deal of potential for the language teacher as it allows presentation and practice of language in a very contextualised manner. Video is easier to handle and more versatile. Video is a very rich and flexible medium capable of conveying both abstract knowledge and concrete examples.

Against these, however, the fact must be acknowledged that the video is still a relatively expensive medium. Access to video equipment is limited and much more cumbersome than sounds and is more demanding on operator time.

FILMS AND SLIDES

Films and slides are teaching aids that can be of a great use in schools to facilitate the teaching/learning process. With films, large classes can be dealt with. Films lighten the task of the teacher as a variety of exciting situations of the outside world are brought into the classroom.

Slides are one of the most useful methods of displaying photographic or graphic images to a class, small group or to individual student. It can be used to facilitate teaching/learning in the primary school classroom. Lessons that are presented through the use of slides can help to develop children's observational power and language.

Despite this importance, schools that have slides do not make good use of them. This is pointed out by Jan (1986) when he says that most modern apparatus such as slides are allowed in schools office shelves gathering dust.

AUDIO OR AURAL AIDS

This category includes all the various systems of instruction whereby straight forward audio signals can be played to, or listened to by, a class, group or individual. It includes a number of extremely useful, albeit often neglected, instructional aids. This category includes, among others, radio and audiotapes.

RADIO

The radio constitutes an extremely useful resource for teachers and pupils. Although it is often difficult to incorporate into the timetable if listened to at the time they are actually transmitted, this can easily be overcome by recording them for later play back.

In most developed countries, the radio has been found to be a valuable instructional material for many children. In some developing countries like Cameroon, the use of the radio has become popular m recent times as most families have been able to afford at least the most inexpensive radio. The radio has a greater advantage of transmitting message since it is portable.

In Cameroon there are few radio programs which are educational such as "KIDS CORNER" which is broadcast over "CRTV" Bamenda every Saturday as from ten o'clock in the morning. Another program called "YOUR WINDOW ON THE WORLD" which is broadcast over "CRTV" national station, every Monday at six o'clock in the evening. Such programs help to develop and improve upon the listening and reading skills of the children.

Such radio programs may be recorded for used at any convenient time. Okorie (1979:147) states that:

> *The pupils should be informed of the time of broadcast*
> *well in advance and should be encouraged to listen to*
> *the program. The programs must relate to the needs*
> *as well as those of general interest. Students should*
> *understand the reason for using radio, what uses will*
> *be made of the programs.*

Radio broadcast must be used m consonance with the appropriate method of teaching. The main disadvantage of the radio, however, is the fixed time of transmission for programs. Learners may be unable to listen to programs at the time they are broadcast. Audiocassettes offer a much greater convenience.

AUDIO TAPES

Audio material recorded on open-reel tape or cassettes constitutes one of the most useful resources at the disposal of the modern teacher and can be used m a wide range of instructional situations either on its own or in conjunction with materials of some sort. Tape recorders are now widely used in primary schools in teaching language. Lessons, discussions, meetings and interviews can be recorded and played back to the children in the classroom at the required moment sounds, notes, noise, speeches or music.

Hedge (1985, p. 100) states that:

161

*Cassettes are useful aids to students reading at home.
The dramatization of a story with different voices and
sound effects or an expensive narration can assist
comprehension considerably. Teachers should suggest
various methods of using a cassette and should advise
students to vary these materials so that motivation is
sustained. Students can be prepared by listening to a
cassette first and then following in their books.*

In using any teaching aid, be it concrete objects, audio visual or aural, one should not however, only consider the content and form of teaching. Emphasis must be placed on the kind of learning skills to be developed, for example motor skills, comprehension, problem solving, interpersonal skills etc. Certain media are better than others in terms of how they represent objects, facts, ideas, processes and their potential to develop learning skills. Text is particularly good for rule-based knowledge, for which there are correct answers or procedures. Video materials are particularly good for procedural and interpersonal skills and for conveying complex, real-life situation that require interpretation. Radio and television are important for listening, reading and arithmetical skills.

METHODOLOGY

POPULATION OF STUDY

The target population of this study was made up of all Anglophone primary school teachers and pupils in Cameroon. The accessible population was made up of all class six pupils and teachers of English Bilingual Primary schools, in Yaounde in the center province.

SAMPLE AND SAMPLING TECHNIQUE

The sample of this study was made up of four of the six Anglophone schools in Yaounde city. The four schools that were selected were: Parents National Educational Union (PNEU), Holy Infant School (HIS), A Government Central English Primary School IV (GCEPSIV), and Government Central English Primary School III (GCEPSIII).

SAMPLING TECHNIQUE

162

As obtained from the Provincial Delegation of National Education, the total number of Anglophone primary schools in Yaounde was six, for the 1996/1997 academic year. The probability sampling technique was used so as to enable all the schools to have equal and independent chance of being selected. Four schools were studied. There were all together seventy 4wo teachers found in the four schools that were selected. Because of the fact that this number was small, we decided to study all the teachers. From the four schools constituting the sample, two groups were formed such that the number of pupils were equal. One group was considered the experimental while the other was the control group.

INSTRUMENTATION

Only one set of questionnaire was used, teachers' questionnaire. The questions consisted mainly of closed-ended questions, since they were required to indicate the right answers by marking from a set of alternatives. The questions asked in the questionnaire were in relation to the research hypotheses that were constructed. The questions were short, clear and simple.

EXPERIMENTATION

An experiment was carried out on the two groups of pupils that were selected to measure the effects of the frequent use of teaching aids on the pupils' performance. Prior to the experiment, a pre-test was set and administered to pupils in both the control group and the experimental groups in the various schools to assess if there was any significant difference m performance between the two groups. Four days after pre-testing, the experimental group was taught a lesson in Rural Science using a combination of visual aids (simple objet) and audio aid (radio cassette). The lesson that was taught to the two groups was the "GRASSHOPPER", an insect The control group was taught the lesson without teaching aids. After a total of four hours (one hour for each school), a common post-test was set and administered to both groups to see if there were any significant differences in the results.

TECHNIQUES OF DATA ANALYSIS

Data collected were presented in tables, charts and graphs. The students' Z test was used to analyze and test the hypotheses.

PRESENTATION OF RESULTS

163

RESULTS OF THE TEACHERS' QUESTIONNAIRE

TABLE 1: The return rate

School	questionnaire distributed		questionnaire returned		Return rate
	male	female	male	female	
PNEU	8	19	8	17	92.6%
GCEPS IV	1	10	1	10	100%
HIS	5	7	4	7	91.7%
GCEPS III	4	18	3	18	95.5%
Total		72		68	94.4%

TABLE 2: The frequency of teaching aids used

Frequency Teaching aids	Always	Once in a while	rarely	Total
Visual aids	37	3	2	42
Audio visual aids	1	4	1	6
Audio aids	0	14	6	20
Total	38	21	9	68

TABLE 3: Types and sources of teaching aids used

teaching aids sources	visual aids	audio visual aids	audio aids	Total
I buy	0	0	15	15
I beg	1	2	3	6
I borrow	2	0	0	2
School provides	10	4	2	16
I make them	29	0	0	29
Total	42	6	20	68

164

STUDENTS' RESULTS

TABLE 4: Combined pre-test scores for the control Group (CG)

x	f	fx	fx2
14	1	14	196
13	7	91	1183
12	3	36	432
11	4	44	484
10	11	110	1100
9	4	36	324
8	2	16	128
7	3	21	147
6	3	18	108
5	6	30	150
4	2	8	32
3	4	12	36
Total	50	436	4320
$X_e=8.72$	$S2_e=10.57$	**$SD_e=3.25$**	$N_e=50$

TABLE 5 Combined pre-test score for the Experimental Group (EG)

x	f	fx	fx2
14	1	14	196
13	5	65	845
12	7	84	1008
11	1	11	121
10	10	100	1000
9	8	17	648
8	3	24	192
7	1	7	49
6	3	18	108
5	4	20	100
4	3	12	48
3	4	12	36
Total	50	439	4351
$X_e=8.78$	$S2_e=10.13$	$SD_e=3.18$	$N_e=50$

Table 6: Combined post-test scores for the Control Group (CG)

x	f	fx	fx2
20	1	20	400
19	1	19	361
18	6	108	1944
17	1	17	289
16	3	48	768
15	7	105	1575
14	5	70	980
13	3	39	507
12	5	60	720
11	2	22	242
10	6	60	600
9	4	36	324
8	2	16	128
6	1	6	36
5	3	15	75
Total	50	641	8949
Xe=12.82	S2e=14.93	SDe=3.86	Ne=50

TABLE 7: Combined post-test scores for the experimental group (EG)

x	f	fx	fx2
20	4	80	1600
19	6	114	2166
18	4	72	1296
17	3	51	867
16	4	64	1024
15	6	90	1350
14	2	28	392
13	4	52	676
12	3	36	432
11	4	44	484
10	5	50	500

9	2	18	162
8	1	8	64
7	2	14	98
Total	50	721	11111
Xe=14.42	S2e=14.58	SDe=3.81	Ne=50

INTERPRETATION AND DISCUSSION OF RESULTS

ATTITUDE OF TEACHERS AS SHOWN BY THE TEACHERS' QUESTIONNAIRE

The majority of teachers indicated that they frequently use visual aids in the course of teaching. This is shown by the fact that 61.6 % of the teacher population frequently used visual aids. Regarding the frequency of usage of the visual aids, 54 % of the population said they use them always. This is evident in table 2. From table 3 the visual aids are mostly used. These aids can be obtained by making them locally or can be bought cheaply. Also, the longer the teachers stay in service, the more they develop the habit of creating and using such simple visual aids.

The first research question could be answered, since the response "always" carries on table 2 55.9 %. It means that teachers in primary school use teaching aids frequently in the course of teaching. But the response "always" was only given more m respect to visual aids. This is affirmed by Stones (1966) by saying that more skill has been done as far as audio visual and audio aids are concerned.

PERFORMANCE OF PUPILS AS SHOWN BY THEIR TEST SCORES

Prior to the experiment pre-test scores of the pupils in the experimental and control groups were collected. The mean performance of the EG was 8.78 and that of the CG was 8.72. Analyzing these scores statistically the results proved that, using the students' Z test, Z calculated was less than Z critical value, 0.09 < 1 65 at df (p)=0.05 using the one tail-test. This shows that the two groups (EG and CG) were at about the same level before the experiment.

The experiment was then conducted by teaching two lessons in each group. The EG was taught using teaching aids and CG was taught without

167

teaching aids. The two groups were given the same post-test. The mean performance of 14.42 for the EG as against 12.82 for the CG showed that the EG performed better than the CG in the post-test. The students' Z calculated for the post-test was 2.71, which was greater than Z critical value which was 1.65 at 0.05 level of significance for a one tail-test and a sample size of 100. Following this results our hypotheses were withheld. Students taught using visual aids and audio aids will perform better than those taught without such aids. This demonstrated clearly by the fact that the highest score for the experimental group rose from 14/20 with a frequency of one to 20/20 with a frequency of 4.

The above analysis and decision, therefore, answer the second research question by indicating that the use of teaching aids improves upon the academic performance of primary school pupils.

SUMMARY OF THE MAJOR FINDINGS

The majority of primary school teachers frequently use only simple visual aids such as simple objects, sketch maps and pictures in the course of teaching. Primary school teachers underestimate the importance of electrically operated teaching aids such as television, video, computers, slides and radio. Schools which have the electrically operated teaching aids do not make fill' use of them. They tend to store them in office shelves gathering dust. Teaching aids, when effectively used, help to clarify instruction. Effective use of teaching aids improves upon the academic performance of primary school pupils.

CONCLUSION

The impression should not be conveyed that every teacher of children in primary schools can succeed without employing educational teaching aids effectively. The research findings were not encouraging. Most of the teachers were tilted towards the use of simple visual aids in the course of teaching. Only few teachers manifested the intention of using audio visual and audio aids in the course of teaching, and they did not even use them regularly or frequently. The frequent use of all types of teaching aids needs to be encouraged in primary schools. Educational planners need to make greater efforts principally in the production of greater number of teaching materials and , especially in training in the use media generally. This is because, as Lockwood (1994) said, learning is likely to be more effective if there are permanent materials such as books, maps, cassettes, video, television, computer and other teaching aids with which learners can interact rather than just ephemeral events like lectures and broadcasts. The frequent use of teaching aids in the course of teaching invites learners to ask and respond to questions or to question or to undertake activities. In fact, effective and frequent use of teaching aids in the course of teaching makes teaching/learning to be learner-centered rather than being teacher-centered as in the case of mere lectures.

References

Barrie, G., & Jill, L. (1990). Children and television: the one eyed monster? London & New York: Routledge.

Farrant, J. (1980). Principles and practice of education London, England: New Edition, Longman hrp UK Ldt.

Gower, R., & Steve, W. (1983). Teaching practice handbook. London: Heinemann Educational Books, Ltd.

Jan, S. (1986). The making of the primary school. Buckingham, Philadelphia: Open University Press.

Luma, L. (1983). The education of African teachers. Yaounde, Cameroon: SOPECAM

Mills, H. (1977). Planning and using the blackboard. Oxford: Heinemann Pub.

Okorie, J. (1979) Fundamentals of teaching Practice. Nigeria: Fourth Dimension Pub. Ce. Ltd .

Stones, E (1966). Introduction to educational psychology. Ibadan, Nigeria: Spectrum Books Ltd .

Tricia, H. (1985). Using readers in language teaching. London, England: Macmillan.

APPENDIX A

QUESTIONNAIRE FOR TEACHERS

Dear teacher:

This exercise is purely academic. Its' purpose is to find out how often you use teaching aids in course of teaching and their effects on pupils' academic performance. Teaching aids are objects or devices used to facilitate the teaching/learning process. Be as objective as possible in answering the questions since there is anonymity.

A/ GENERAL INFORMATION

School

Class

Sex

B/ Mark "X" on the line that corresponds to the right answer.

1: What is your qualification?

__Grade I   __Grade II   __Grade III

2: For how long have you been teaching in this school?

__10-5 years   __16-10 years   __Above 10 years

3:

a: Do you use visual aids in the course of teaching?

__Yes   __No

b: Which of them do you use?

__Wallsheets   __Simple objects   __Posters

__Not at all   __None   __All

c: How often do use them?

__Always   __Once in a while

__Rarely   __Not at all

4.

a: Do you use audio aids in the course of teaching?

__Yes   __No

b: Which of them do you use?

__Television   __Films

__Slides   __Computers

c: How often do you use them?

__Always   __Once in a while

__Rarely   __Not at all

6: How do you get your teaching aids?

__I buy   __I beg   __I borrow

__School provides   __I make

7: How often do you ask your pupils to bring teaching aids to school?

__Always   __Once in a while

__Rarely   __Not at all

8: Which teaching aids do you think are more effective in terms of children's performance?

__Visual aids   __Audio aids   __Audio/Visual aids

9: When using teaching aids, how do your pupils behave?

__They participate actively.

__They listen quietly.

__They make noise.

__They do not care.

10: Do you often evaluate your pupils using teaching aids?

__Yes   __No

PRE-TEST

RURAL SCIENCE   DURATION: 20 minutes

Answer all the following questions carefully on a neat sheet of paper. Do not copy from your friends.

1: List two common insects that are found in your house sheet.   2 marks

2: Name two insects that are harmful to our crops.   2 marks

3: Name two common insects that can be used as food.   2 marks

4: Name two insects that cause or transmit human diseases.   2 marks

5: Name two common parts of an insect.   2 marks

ANSWERS

1: Cockroach, mosquitoes, spider, etc.
2: Locust, termites, yam beetles grasshopper, aphids, etc.
3: Locust, termites, bamboo beetle, etc.
4: flies, mosquitoes, lice, jiggers, etc.

5: Head, legs, wings, mouth, eyes, etc.

CHAPTER 16

GUIDANCE AND COUNSELING: HAS IT FAILED OUR STUDENTS?

Glenda Smith Starr, Masters' +30
Assistant Professor
Department of Teacher Education
College of Education
Grambling State University
Grambling, LA

The guidance department in elementary and secondary public schools and in universities is the focus of student personnel services. The main purpose of this department is to personalize and humanize the educational process. Given the vast scope of responsibilities that this department continues to accumulate, it is doubtful that it can truly fulfill its purpose as an entity which should be available throughout the entire school system.

In the elementary and secondary schools the teachers often assume the role of guidance counselor This is probably because the teacher is more apt to form a relationship with students than the guidance counselor. Usually, the guidance office is the scheduling and testing center Only those students with extremely special concerns go to the counselor's office to discuss personal situations. Many elementary schools do not have guidance counselors and teachers have no choice but to accommodate the needs and concerns if students. Secondary school guidance is centered around more academic counseling than student concerns. Where do students who have problems that are not adequately addressed in the home turn? It should be to the school guidance counselor but usually this is not true. Has guidance and counseling in schools failed our students?

Dinkmeyer and Caldwell (1988) write that the current situation in higher education demands serious study of the crucial need for guidance. Students from all age groups, backgrounds and experiences enter the university level. Most of them are in dire need of counseling Some are returning adults, some are veterans and some are non-traditional women who need guidance toward adjusting their lives with academic schedules. Guidance as a function provides the personal concern that students will need to become actively engaged as a learner and a functional citizen in an active society Guidance, also, assists in making individualized and personally meaningful instruction a reality. Guidance is that part of the education program which emphasizes the individual Is our guidance and counseling department in our schools, on any level, meeting these needs of students?

Guidance departments should help students to develop and establish purposes and goals and think in terms of choice Emphasis should be on development of competence in the student competence in this sense refers to academic achievement, knowledge, values, skills, attitudes and feelings which contribute to the student's mastery in learning If the guidance department is fulfilling these needs, then, indeed the guidance and counseling department is failing to meet the needs of our students.

In order for guidance to be effective, it must be more than an office visit, a group experience, a diagnostic appraisal, or any other function by the specialist. The guidance philosophy must permeate the entire structure of the school system to the extent that it influences the administration, the practices of the classroom teachers, and the daily learning of the student. Guidance and counseling must have a total impact on the life of the student or the life of the student or it will ultimately cause failure and incompleteness of existence.

References

Dinkmeyer, D., & Caldwell, E. (1988). <u>Guidance and counseling: A comprehensive school approach</u>. New York: McGraw-Hill.

CHAPTER 17

COMMUNICATION AMONG STUDENTS, PARENTS, AND TEACHERS IS MISSING A MAIN INGREDIENT... "LISTENING SKILLS"

Glenda Smith Starr, Masters' +30
Assistant Professor
Department of Teacher Education
College of Education
Grambling State University
Grambling, LA

Listening is the most difficult of all the communication skills to master. Why? Is it because this is one skill that we have never truly been trained to learn to effectively apply? When people tail to listen, at least one other communication skill suffers. Certainly, speaking is null and void without having anyone to listen. Both of these skills are essential to communication. Communication among students, parents and teacher appears to be missing a main ingredient - "Listening Skills".

If students, parents and teachers don't start listening to each other, the educational system is going to be in trouble. Children need parents to hear their concerns about school and what kind of day that they **really** had. Parents, also, need their children to hear about the school-day experiences. There just **might** be a lesson to be learned in those frequently told stories. Teachers need to listen to their students and vice versa in order to improve the teaching and learning cycle.

It is easy to get caught up in the big picture issues in education, such as grades or the even bigger picture, such as teachers salaries, but without communication, especially listening skills, there will be no cause and effect. To acquire the skill of listening is worth celebrating, and children, parents and teachers must all become competent participants in this celebration.

Today teachers and parents are concerned about students learning to think and solve problems which cannot be achieved if listening is not maximized. Listening is a main ingredient John Bransford (1996) indicates in his Teaching Thinking and Problem Solving that listening is a skill which must be developed at an early age. It is indeed a skill which must continuously be built on through a lifetime. Assessment of student achievement suggest that today's students may be failing to develop effective thinking and problem solving skills because prior

179

listening skills have not been developed. Since the goal of teaching, thinking and problem solving is not unique, it is necessary to include the importance of a main ingredient which is listening. Previous studies during the 1970s and 1980s have generally emphasized "mental discipline" and the active ingredient underlying effective thinking and problem solving Could this "mental discipline" be synonymous with "listening"?

Mastery of listening also include the concept of metacognition. Researchers who have studies differences in approaches to learning have tried to work with materials that require knowledge that is potentially available to participants. Bransford (1996) also explains that the goal of research has assessed the degree to which people spontaneously utilize knowledge previously acquired Results have led to a number of researchers to argue that people's ability to use what they know and to access task-relevant information is an important hallmark of intelligence. The extent of which depends largely on their listening skills. The metacognitive approach to teaching and to communication among students, parents, and teachers may possibly help them to improve their abilities to listen, think and learn in a wide variety of domains. The types of early social environments facilitate the development of listening skills that enable children to learn in formal educational setting.

Students, parents and teachers alike are aware of a continuous acquisition toward "higher order" skills within the learning process. Varying theories of access should provide an important framework for helping students to listen, learn to think and solve problems. Repeatedly, orators state "Parents are teachers, too" and this extended role includes the statement, "Parents are listeners, too." Collectively, students, parents and teachers must include and observe the missing ingredient in communication... "Listening Skills".

References

Bransford, J., & Others. (1996, October). Teaching thinking and problem solving. American Psychologist, 41(10). The American Psychological Association.

CHAPTER 18

CRUCIAL DISADVANTAGES FACING "AT-RISK" POPULATIONS OF YOUNG ADULTS IN TODAY'S SOCIETY

Glenda Smith Starr, Masters' +30
Assistant Professor
Department of Teacher Education
College of Education
Grambling State University
Grambling, LA

Donald W. Smith, Ed.D.
Principal, Wossman High School
Monroe City Schools
Monroe, LA

What constitutes an "At-Risk'" population? Is this distinction based solely upon the economically advantaged, is this distinction based largely upon excessive devisive disciplinary behavior or is there any evidence that this distinction is based upon race or ethnic characteristics? Then, the question may occur. - At risk of what? When readers see at-risk with regards to social problems, there is an immediate concern that someone is a candidate for diversion from the norm of societal standards. That person has also displayed some tendencies to indicate a path toward a life of crime or an ill-fated journey of turbulence.

Perhaps, poverty does contribute to the at-risk state of being. When people exist in poverty, there is a certain degree of desirability. At the same time there is also a void or loss for missing luxuries which are essentials for others. Due to environmental factors discipline problems occur when these people have occasions to interact with other facets of society. Without being intentional, race or ethnic characteristics do come into play when there is a distinction of an at-risk population. The minorities are usually the ones who are "at-risk'" because they have not been privy to those in life that make other people considered as **"not** at-risk".

Within the population of the at-risk are young adults, ages 18-22 who have some crucial disadvantages as they attempt to find their place in society If they have reached this age without being incarcerated and still alive, then they have to be prepared to enter into the world of work and to adjust and fit in with the rest of society. In the job market references will not come easy. In fact, it will be quite difficult to prove themselves as deserving reputable employees.

As they venture into other neighborhoods, they will also have to produce more than the rent in order to prove themselves worthy for better housing. opportunities Often these young adults have existed in neighborhoods that have not represented the living style comparable to the "across the track" counterparts. They have to learn the value of household maintenance and occupancy. Yet, they do deserve an opportunity to prove themselves.

During these years they will still have to survive peer pressure. Unfortunately, many of the other 15 to 22 year olds with whom they grew up may not have taken the big step to get beyond their childhood stigma. Peer pressure can bring temptation of illicit behavior, drugs and crime, all of which may project "fast and easy money". On the other hand peers may press the point, "Don't forget your roots." If they are to become productive citizens in the world in which they live, they must survive and ignore this type of negative pressure.

Maeroff (1998) points out that the struggle to build social capital for at risk young people represents one of the most important endeavors in the country today. Lacking such an edge, this group of young adults can barely get a toehold as they attempt to climb out of poverty. The network of connections that ties them to success in quite limited. When these young adults gain a sense of connectedness to people and institutions in society whose guidance and assistance will direct them toward advancing themselves, they will began to feel more secure with fewer disadvantages to cope with from day to day

There are crucial disadvantages for young adults, ages 18-22, as they make attempts to enter into the world of work and take on responsibilities. However, they cannot become discouraged because they hold the key to their own future. It is their responsibility to assure their offspring a more productive future and to make sure that their children will be rescued from the "at-risk' population of the future.

References

Maeroff, G. I. (1998). Altered destinies. Phi Delta Kappan, 79(8), pp. 425-426

CHAPTER 19

A TEACHER-TRAINING MODEL FOR PROMOTING EDUCATION THAT IS MULTICULTURAL THROUGH TELECOMMUNICATION

Loretta Walton Jaggers, Ed.D.
Associate Professor
Department of Teacher Education
College of Education
Grambling State University
Grambling, LA

Vicki Renee Brown, Ph.D.
Principal, Grambling Middle Magnet School
Associate Professor
College of Education
Grambling State University
Grambling, LA

Introduction

This chapter is designed to present content, activities/strategies. materials which may be used in a teacher training program to demonstrate "how to" incorporate multicultural processes across the curriculum. Strategies, activities, and materials which are used to promote "education that is multicultural" at Grambling Middle Magnet will also be presented as a "success" model. Grambling Middle Magnet School is one of the Laboratory Schools at Grambling State University (Louisiana).

This instructional model was designed for a graduate level telecommunications course in the Teacher Education Department which was offered through the Center for Distance Learning at Grambling State University. This course, ED 525: Trends and Strategies in Multi-Ethnic Education, was designed to cover a twelve week period for two hours and fifty minutes per week. The focus of the course was to first, promote an awareness and understanding of the goals and background of multicultural education and the underlying philosophy of cultural pluralism. Secondly, emphasis was placed on current trends and strategies in multicultural education which may be used to enhance the teaching-learning process. Thirdly, attention was given to the development of activities, strategies and materials (commercial and non-commercial) for incorporating the concept of multicultural education into the existing curriculum. Finally, the role of the school, the community, and the administration in promoting the philosophy of cultural pluralism was also presented. Opportunities were provided for interactive discussions with educational experts in the field of multicultural education, curriculum development, and teacher education. The presentation of classroom activities, and materials from the Grambling Middle Magnet School served to demonstrate specific activities, strategies, learning environments, materials/resources, attitudes and behaviors for promoting education that in multicultural across the curriculum.

Rationale

Many leading experts in the field of multicultural education have expressed a continuous need for the educational system to meet the diverse populations of students through the use of content, activities, materials, and processes which promote education that is mulitcultural. Specifically, Fillmore indicates that due to the "diverse multicultural" society m which we live, there is a need for educators and community leaders to work together to provide classroom experiences which enable children to "acquire the means and desire to build a society in which diverse people live together harmoniously and at peace with one another" (Fillmore, 1993). In order to be able to provide these experiences for students, there must be structured preservice and in-service training programs and courses for teachers, administrators, and community leaders.

These structured experiences must first include in-depth discussions of the history and philosophical base of multicultural education. There must also be some clarification of multicultural education as related to practical application. This phase is very important because Banks indicates that over the past years, there have been some serious misconceptions about "theory and practice in multicultural education which have reduced the outstanding accomplishments that have been made in the area (Banks, J., 1993). These training experiences must also include activities for involving parents, community representatives, and educators in collaborative efforts to enhance the teaching-learning process. Banks indicted that through effective parent and teacher interaction, students have an opportunity to improve academic achievement and success (13anks, C.,1993;) Additionally, the training experiences must provide opportunities for students to identify, discuss, and compare the five approaches to multicultural education as outlined by Grant and Sleeter, 1996. This process provides an opportunity for

188

educators to become more knowledgeable of each approach so that they may identify and apply appropriate strategies and materials to classroom instruction.

Specific instructional strategies, activities and materials are very important elements to be included in planning and organizing multicultural educational training programs. Teachers must be able to utilize the students' background experiences to teach new concepts (Willis 1993). Teachers must use varied instructional strategies to meet the diverse needs and learning styles of students. Educators must also be able to observe and discuss existing programs and materials that have had positive results. Based on the literature review, the instructional model was designed to provide background information about multicultural education, present specific strategies for classroom implementation, and discuss the role of the administration, the community/parent, and the school in the implementation process.

Instructional Design

Overview

The course was designed to provide a variety of activities, materials using transparencies, video productions, and presentations by experts in multicultural education, curriculum development and teacher education. One of the highlights of the telecourse was the presentation made by Dr. Carl Grant, the author of the text which was used for the course. Dr. Grant's presentation focused on the role of the community in promoting education that is multicultural. He used specific illustrations and examples as he discussed a community involvement model which was included in one of his publication. This experience also provided opportunities for the students to ask questions and further interact with the author about concepts presented and discussed in the textbook.

The course instructor, Dr. Loretta Walton Jaggers, Associate Professor of Education at Grambling State University, designed the course especially for the telecommunications presentation. She planned and facilitated activities so that each session included creative and interesting strategies that encouraged students to call in and interact. She also used a variety of transparencies that included illustrations and charts to express concepts and ideas discussed or presented in the text. The special guest consultants served to diversify and add strength to the course as they discussed their area of expertise in relation to multicultural education. Each class session started with a presentation of the agenda, which included a review of content from the last class, outlined activities for the present class period and assignments for the following class period. During each class period, students called in to discuss assignments and ask questions. Students mailed in assignments and received feedback from the course instructor and special guest consultants. Each session was videotaped.

Objectives

The following are the performance objectives to be achieved:

Obj. 1:   Explore the philosophy of cultural pluralism.

Obj. 2:   Articulate definitions of selected concepts central to an adequate understanding of the multicultural/multi-ethnic phenomena.

Obj. 3:   List and explain some procedures for incorporating the concept into a given content area (K-12).

Obj. 4:   a.   Construct a lesson and a teacher-made device with interrelates a given content area with the goals of multicultural education.
            b.   Design a multicultural teaching aid to be used as an introduction, complement, support or culminating part of a given lesson.

Obj. 5:   View and discuss a mediated presentation entitled, "Multicultural Education: An Overview".

Obj. 6:   Evaluate some instructional materials (textbooks, kits, teaching aides, etc.) to determine the existence of stereotyping and the treatment of culturally diverse students.

Obj. 7:   Discuss the role of affective skills in the implementation of
             multicultural education.

Obj. 8:   Identify some of the major issues in cultural and ethnic patterns of
             communication that impact learning. These include verbal,
             nonverbal, and transracial dimensions of communication.

Obj. 9:   Critique and critically discuss articles on multicultural education as
             a result of extensive research.

Obj.10:   Develop an annotated bibliography of current references related to
             multicultural education.

Obj.11:   Discuss the role of the teacher, the administration, and the
             community in institutionalizing multicultural education.

Activities

The following activities are intended to meet the stated goals and objectives:

+   Evaluate instructional materials for the treatment of students from diverse
      cultures.

+   Reaction Papers: Write 5 reaction papers to current journal articles from
      literature dealing with the impact of culture, race, ethnicity and socio
      economic status on the educational process.

+   Annotated Bibliography: Compile an annotated bibliography of 10 current
      references dealing with the impact of culture, race, ethnicity and socio
      economic status on the educational process.

+   Project: Select and redesign one component of school curriculum to reflect
      the multicultural focus and include culturally responsive teacher materials
      that are developed by the student during the semester.

Implementation of Teacher-Training
Model for Promoting Education That Is Multicultural at
Grambling Middle Magnet School

Overview

Grambling State University Laboratory Middle Magnet School is a campus-based facility located in Grambling, Louisiana. The school plan is designed for students of grades 6th-8th in a departmentalized structure. Students come from Lincoln Parish and surrounding parishes who seek accelerated educational opportunities beyond the bounds of the "traditional" classroom setting. Its purpose then and now, was to provide for the educational needs of the children in this area and to support the program in Teacher Education at Grambling State University, Grambling, Louisiana.

The middle school makes up a department in the College of Education, Grambling, Louisiana, and is dedicated to supporting and advancing the purposes and goals of the university. The primary role of the middle school is to provide a model program of education to its students and to develop, evaluate, and disseminate exemplary programs of education to other schools.

Thus, my task today is to provide the audience with an increased awareness and understanding of innovative techniques, strategies, and materials in multi-ethnic education that are used at Grambling Middle Magnet School (GMMS) to enhance the teaching learning process. The strength of our school has its foundation in the broad support we give and receive in the teacher-training model. Imbedded in this model are several components that provide for a balance of academic goals and other human development needs of early adolescents.

Description of Model

Realizing the importance of high achievement in the basic skills and exhibiting high expectations for student performance, teachers at Grambling Middle Magnet School are expected to teach a variety of learning styles, abilities, beliefs, ethnic backgrounds, personal interests and family problems. Thus, to transform our school so that African-American students could experience success

192

and an equal opportunity to learn in school, multicultural infusion was the vehicle in helping our students find a place in the pluralistic world. Stereotyping, resegregating, tracking, indoctrinating and assigning blame on the student, teacher, parent, community resources, etc. was avoided. Moreover, our teachers have a command of what they need to do in their classrooms based on the problems of diversity they confront. Our teachers understand the importance of:

1. caring about and respecting all children
2. teaching them to care about each other
3. showing them that hatred hurts
4. showing them how to be critical thinkers
5. showing them how to believe in themselves
6. challenging all students academically
7. boosting their self-image appreciating family ties throughout generations
8. offering them new worlds to discover as well as the tools to change, and
9. creating a caring community in the school and even a smaller one in classrooms.

The major thrust or frame of the model is the home and the school joined by team support, i.e. the big three; school, home, community. Imbedded in the school involves the principal, faculty, staff, parents/community working together as a team to ensure that numerous procedures and a variety of diverse content are used to enhance the academic success of African-American youth. In a nutshell, the team shares some common beliefs to include the following:

1) Real learning is unlikely to occur unless students feel accepted first by students and teacher (Maslow), and

2) If America is to reclaim its youth, educators must help children establish a healthy self-esteem by getting them to act independently, assume responsibility, be proud of accomplishments, especially within their culture, and approach new challenges with enthusiasm.

References

Angell, P. et al. (1993). Celebrating diversity. Learning '93, 21(6), 61-68.

Banks, C. (1993). Restructuring schools for equity: What we have learned in two decades. Phi Delta Kappan, 75(1), 42-49.

Banks, J. (1993). Multicultural education: Development dimensions and challenges. Phi Delta Kappan, 75(1), 22-28.

Banks, J. A. (1991, December/1992, January). Multicultural education: For freedom's sake. Educational Leadership, 32-36.

Cooperative learning. (1992, September). Instructor, 102(2).

Duhon-Sells, R. (1992). Multicultural education for the twenty-first century. In C. Grant (Ed.), Proceedings of the Second Annual Meeting (NAME) (pp. viii- x). Morristown, NJ: Paramount Publishing.

Fillmore, L. (1993). Educating citizens for a multicultural 21st century. Multicultural Education, 1(1), 10-12.

Gomez, A. (1992, December). Multicultural crafts. Instructor, 102(4).

Grant, C., & Sleeter, C. (1988). Making choices for multicultural education: Five approaches to race. class. and gender. New York: Macmillan Publishing Co.

Grant, C. & Sleeter, C. (1989). Turning on learning: Five approaches for multicultural teaching plans for race. class. gender. and disability. New York: Macmillan.

Hemandez, H. (1989). Multicultural education: A teacher's guide to content and process. Columbus: Merrill Publishing Company.

History's other voice. (1992, September). Instructor, 102(2).

Jones-Agard, L. (1993). Implementing multicultural education: The New York city experience. Multicultural Education, 1(1), 13-15.

Multicultural reviews. (1993). Multicultural Education, 1(1), 31-39.

Sleeter, C. (1992). Keepers of the American dream: A study of staff development and multicultural education. Washington, DC: The Falmer Press.

194

Smith, G. P. (1993). Multicultural resources. <u>Multicultural Education, 1</u>(1), 25-30.

Willis, S. (1993, September). Multicultural teaching: Meeting the challenge that arise in practice. <u>Curriculum Update</u>. Association for the Supervision of Curriculum Development.

MULTI-ETHNIC / MULTICULTURAL EDUCATION

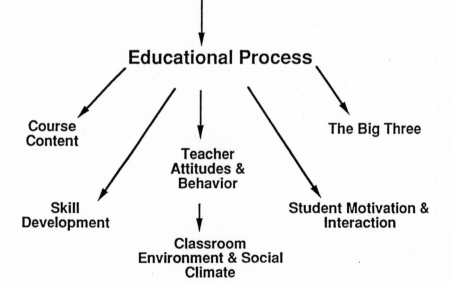

The Philosophy of Cultural Pluralism

Educational Process

Course Content

Teacher Attitudes & Behavior

The Big Three

Skill Development

Student Motivation & Interaction

Classroom Environment & Social Climate

Jaggers/1992

CHAPTER 20

CARE: A MODEL FOR DEVELOPING
EFFECTIVE LIFE-LONG DECISION MAKING SKILLS

Loretta Walton-Jaggers, Ed.D.
Associate Professor
Department of Teacher Education
College of Education
Grambling State University
Grambling, LA

In today's society there is an increasing number of students that are involved in violent and criminal acts. Specifically, many youth across the country are involved in gang activity, drugs, "car jacking", robbery, murder and many other violent crimes. Since these youngsters are to be the "leaders of tomorrow," it becomes necessary to identify possible factors which may cause or impact these negative behaviors which are exhibited. According to a review of the literature many negative behaviors result from a lack of positive self-concept and a need to belong or be accepted by family and peers. The literature further indicates that self-esteem is a crucial element toward academic achievement and success. Therefore, when students continuously lack positive feelings of self and continuously experience failure, then they may act out negatively or become involved in individual or group activity which is against the laws of society. Therefore, there is a need for the curriculum to promote numerous opportunities for students to experience success. There also must be opportunities for students to develop and expand self-esteem through the use of varied strategies, techniques, materials, and activities. This provides opportunities for students to discuss feelings, attitudes and emotions while developing productive life-long decision making skills and strengthening overall academic skills.

Such experiences can be reflected through the incorporation of Affective Education into the instructional process. Affective Education is an educational process which provides direct and indirect experiences which allows students to develop and expand positive feelings of self and others, explore attitudes and emotions, clarify values, and make responsible choices. Through the direct incorporation of affective activities into the curriculum, students will have a greater opportunity to develop an increased awareness understanding and respect for self an others while learning to make responsible choices. Additionally, this

197

technique would also promote improved oral and written communicative skills as well as overall academic achievement.

Based on the foregoing, the CARE Model appears to offer many opportunities for students to explore and expand affective skills which are needed to develop effective and productive life-long decision-making skills; and possibly help to alleviate negative behavior and acts of crime and violence. It is also mandatory for the CARE Model to be incorporated into the K-12 curriculum. Additionally, in an effort to promote the success of such a program, it is necessary to have appropriate staff development programs which involve intensive training, "hands-on" experiences, and continuous follow-up and feedback during the implementation process.

The CARE Model: A Description

Based on the expressed need reflected in the literature review and the statistics of criminal incidents in today's society, the CARE Model provides opportunities for students to develop positive self-concepts, clarify values, and utilize "dispute resolution" strategies for problem solving, as they develop effective life-long decision-making skills. Additionally, through the utilization of such a model, students will have an increased opportunity to strengthen basic cognitive skills such as reading, thinking, listening, speaking, and writing skills which are necessary for overall success in school and life. This Model is designed to be incorporated into the existing K-1 2 curriculum. CARE basically demonstrates a sense of caring or concern for self and others as related to making appropriate and responsible choices. Specifically, the components of the Model include the following:

C-The C represents "Communication". This phase provides an opportunity for students to become involved in numerous cooperative learning activities involving small group discussions. These activities should include "dispute resolution" experiences where students can use realistic situations or issues to discuss and make choices based on alternatives and consequences. Varied creative communication activities provides increased self-awareness as well as respect of the "rights" of others. A variety of human and material resources may be utilized (e.g., community consultants, periodicals, school related situations).

A-The A represents "Attitude Control". This phase provides opportunities for students to be involved in numerous activities which provides opportunities to identify elements of positive and negative attitudes as related to making choices and handling situations rationally. This phase also involves the discussion of values clarification in relation to effective decision-making skills. This phase will involve active participation through role play, small group interaction, and reactions to mediated presentations (e.g., videos, slides, filmstrips).

R-The B represents "Resolution Dispute". This step is designed to include a variety of assigned readings and discussions which allow students to "resolve" specific heated issues using rational decision-making strategies. Emphasis will be placed on a systematic problem-solving approach. Opportunities will be provided for students to apply the "systematic approach" to realistic situations.

E-The E represents "Esteem Development". Since self-esteem and the need for acceptance or belonging appears to be the basis of much of the negative behavior exhibited by youth. Self-esteem development must be a crucial component of the model. Specifically, this phase will first include a variety of self-awareness activities for student participation. Students will be involved in (Magic Circle) activities to promote increased self-expression and respect for the opinions of others.

CARE Staff Development: A Conceptual Scheme

Introduction

In order to promote the successful incorporation of the CARE Model into the K-12 curriculum, it is necessary to have a well designed staff development program. This design must include appropriate performance objectives with accompanying "hands-on" activities for teachers, administrators, and paraprofessionals who will be involved in the implementation process. Incentives

199

will be provided for persons who participate in the staff development activities. Specifically, all participants will receive graduate credit and a stipend for active involvement in the series of on-site activities.

Design of the CARE Staff Development Program

The staff development program for CARE is termed the "CARE Inservice Training Workshop". It involves a six week intensive training period which involves a variety of activities which relate to each of the components of the CARE Model. The participants go through the actual activities which are designed for use with the students. Specifically, the tentative general schedule of events follow for the six week period. The participants meet from 9:00a.m. - 12:00 p.m. Monday through Wednesday.

The CARE In-Service Training Workshop

Week I   - Overview Need/Rationale

             - Pre-Assessment Simulated Activities

             - Simulated Activities

Week II   - Direct Instruction

             - Introduction of CARE Model

             Components

             (Part I - Emphasis on C)

                   - Simulated Activities

                   - Mediated Productions

                   - Community Consultants

Week III   - Direct Instruction

             - Continuation of CARE Model

             - Components

             (Part II - Emphasis on A)

                   - Simulated Activities

                   - Mediated Productions

                   - Community Consultants

Week IV   - Direct Instruction

             - Continuation of CARE Model

             Components

	(Part III - Emphasis on R)
	- Simulated Activities
	- Mediated Productions
	- Community Consultants
Week V	- Direct Instruction
	- Continuation of CARE Model
	Components
	(Part IV - Emphasis on E)
	- Simulated Activities
	- Mediated Productions
	- Community Consultants
Week VI	- Post-Assessment
	- Evaluations

Population

The in-service training sessions are designed to be held at one of the Grambling State University Laboratory Schools. The participants are inservice teachers, administrators, and paraprofessionals from selected schools in the Lincoln Parish School System. Consultants that are involved in the session presentations are community leaders in the areas of law enforcement, education, politics, business, and religion. The workshop facilitator is responsible for coordinating the overall events.

Participants are expected to attend and actively participate in each of the sessions during the six week period. The sessions were held during the 1994 summer session. Each participant received a certificate of recognition for their commitment and active involvement in the workshop. Additionally, they received a stipend and credit hours.

The process for identifying participants was on a voluntary basis for teachers in the Lincoln Parish School System. Participants were made aware that they will be expected to return to the original workshop site in the fall and spring semester for periodic follow-up sessions.

Workshop Objectives and Instructional Procedures

Given varied content, activities, and materials, each participant will:

-Explain the need for emphasizing effective life-long decision-making skills in the K-12 curriculum;

201

-Identify the rationale for such a program which relates to the CARE Model;

-List and describe each component of the CARE Model;

-Demonstrate specific strategies, activities and materials which may be used to promote effective decision-making skills;

-Discuss creative techniques for promoting productive decision-making skills according to individual classroom settings.

There is an Instructional Model which is developed by the Workshop Facilitator. This module includes specific performance objectives for each of the sessions. There are also be specific activities that relate to each of the objectives.

The specific objectives relate to the topics presented in the tentative calendar of events which was cited previously. Opportunities are provided for participants to devise their own "involvement activities" so that they will be tailored for the needs and backgrounds of their individual learners. The activities that the participants were involved in were the same activities that the students completed at the individual schools during the 1994-95 school session.

Implementation Team

The workshop implementation team involves the following:

-Program Coordinator

-Workshop Facilitator

-Evaluator (Program)

-Material Production Assistant (Clerical Assistant)

Budgetary Needs

I.   Workshop Staff

    A.   Program Coordinator

    B.   Workshop Facilitator

    C.   Clerical Assistants (2)

    D.   Program Evaluator

II.   Stipend for Participants

    A.   In-Service Teachers

    B.   Administrators

    C.   Paraprofessionals

D. Special National Consultants

III. Production of Resources
   A. Duplication of Materials
   B. Dissemination of Communications

IV. Special Funds (Optional)
   A. Continental Breakfast (1st Session)
   B. Refreshments during Special Community Consultant Presentation

V. Travel
   A. Sites where similar programs are in existence
   B. Conferences where related topics are presented
   C. Local, state, and national conferences to present Model (CARE)

CHAPTER 21

A COMMUNITY-BASED PROGRAM FOR PROMOTING ACADEMIC SKILLS, SELF-ESTEEM, AND CULTURAL AWARENESS

Loretta Walton Jaggers, Ed.D.
Associate Professor
Department of Teacher Education
College of Education
Grambling State University
Grambling, LA

This chapter outlines and describes the basic components of a community enrichment program which was designed to develop and enhance cultural, academic, and life-long learning skills. This chapter includes a description of activities and resources which are used during after-school tutoring sessions and field-based experiences in the larger community.

Louisiana Assistance Program: An Overview

The Louisiana Assistance Program was designed to promote an increased community awareness and growth through the expansion and enhancement of knowledge. Specifically, the program provides opportunities for academic and cultural enrichment, industrial development, and motivation and aid for individuals to obtain and maintain jobs. Support services are also provided for law enforcement officials through various activities which are initiated by the "war-on-crime" component. All activities sponsored by the Louisiana Assistance Programs, Inc. are designed to promote a strong sense of civic pride and responsibility. Additionally, this program was founded on the philosophy of, "prevention, education, and screening -- three keys to a healthy society". As a result, all efforts and activitities provided by the program promote this philosophy.

The Louisiana Assistance Program, Inc. was organized to provide assistance for citizens in Claiborne, Bienville, Lincoln, and Union parishes. The specific cities include, Arcadia, Athens, Bernice, Gibsland, Grambling, Haynesville, Homer, Junction City, Lisbon, Ruston and Simsboro.

The program components include: Cultural Academic Life Training (CAL),War-On-Crime, Senior Services, and Health Awareness, Youth Legislature, Abuse , and Employment Programs. Although there are numerous on-going activities for each of the components, this report will specifically focus on program description and activities for the (Cultural Academic Life Training Component (CAL).

During 1993-94 the focus of the program was on planning, organizing, and designing. Numerous efforts were made to help promote a quality program designed to meet the program objectives and needs of the community,. The implementation of program objectives begun during 1995-96. The model used for program implementation provides numerous opportunities to reflect and review the objectives and activities so that we may expand, delete, and strengthen to better serve the community.

Cultural Academic Life Training Profile

CAL Overview

The Cultural Academic Life (CAL) Training component is designed to develop and enhance cultural, academic, and life-long learning skills necessary for individuals to become productive and successful citizens in an ever-changing society. Specifically, this component is designed to provide assistance and support services (for individuals from five to nineteen years of age) to enhance self-esteem, creativity, self-motivation and academic achievement. This component also provides numerous opportunities and experiences which encourage independent and critical thinking, acceptance of challenges and responsibilities, self-pride and appropriate decision-making strategies. Lastly, this component emphasizes "service" to the community, the nation, and the world. This process involves giving, sharing, exchanging, and interacting with others to help promote an increased awareness, understanding, support, and acceptance of our ever changing society.

Based on the previously stated goals of CAL, there were numerous and varied activities which were on-going at each of the site locations. Some of these activities included (1) classes in drama, dance, arts, and crafts, tutorial sessions, and cultural enrichment programs which provided opportunities for the participants to display their work and present culminating activities for parents and teachers.

Tutorial Sites and Activities
Structure

The tutorial sessions were held at the designated sites after school to provide support services in the academic areas of need. Specifically, the areas whereby services were provided included Math and Reading/Language arts. Each site had a head teacher which is selected
by the Executive Director of the Louisiana Assistance Program. Each Head Teacher was responsible for coordinating the program activities for each tutorial site, keeping records provided by the individual teacher, and ordering and disseminating supplies.

The staff for each site included teachers, aides at some sites and volunteers. Specifically, the teachers for the programs were made up of retired educators, certified teachers presently teaching, university students, and community persons serving as volunteers.

The tutorial sessions were designed for a two hour period after school. During the academic school year, they were scheduled on Monday through Thursday from 4:00 p.m. -6:00 p.m. During the summer they were scheduled from 8:00 a.m. - 2:00 p.m. Monday -Friday. Transportation to the various sites was provided by some of the churches, the Grambling Housing Authority, and sometimes the teachers. The specific focus in many of the sites was to help students with homework assignments, and to increase test scores on the LEAP test (Louisiana Educational Assessment (California Achievement Test).   After students received snacks, then they divided into groups to work on special assignments and activities. The activities varied at the various sites according to the needs of the students.

Instruction

The instruction was based on the both formal and informal assessment. The pre-assessment procedure involves test results from the designated schools in which the student attended, and observation of class performance from the tutorial teachers.   The post-assessment involved informal as well as formal testing at given points of instruction at the tutorial site. Periodic feedback was also obtained from regular school teachers and parents as related to progress of the students.

Teachers used individual lesson plans to organize the instructional objectives as related to the activities and specific evaluation strategies.

Cultural Enrichment Experiences

The students participating in the tutorial sessions also had the opportunity to participate in culminating programs and field trips. These rich experiences provided opportunities for the students to expand their self-esteem, increase communication skills, and increase their knowledge through direct hands-on exposure. Students thoroughly enjoyed these activities because they have an opportunity to "learn new things through doing."

Student Progress Procedures

A student progress report was maintained on each student at the given tutorial site location. The teacher's report included a narrative describing the specific performance and/or included a performance checklist. For example, a Terrill Street Housing Site teacher wrote a report regarding her 1st grade student, "Taylor has done well in tutoring. Her report card grades have increased from 3.33 to 3.67. She likes doing other assignments to challenge herself." (April 1995). A second progress report of a 5th grade student at the same tutorial site, "Jerome is a good student who made a lot of careless mistakes on his work. Since being at tutoring he has raised his grade point average from 3.33 to 3.67. He loves to show us his weekly papers and report card." (April 1995) A third progress report of a 4th grader at the same site, "Shaneque is a good student who was having trouble with long division. Drill and practice with her has helped her quite a bit. She has done better in her school work as a result of this practice." (Jan.1996)

The Carter Memorial Temple Tutorial Site Coordinator sent a letter to the principal/teacher requesting a copy of the student's report cards with the signed permission of the parent. This information helped the tutorial teachers to see how the students are progressing in their regular school classes after exposure to the tutorial sessions. A copy of all of the individual progress reports for each of the tutorial sites were available upon request. Evidence indicated that students definitely benefitted from the exposure to the tutorial sessions which were designed to meet the individual needs.

Attendance Reporting and Procedures

Each student was required to complete a "Registration form" to officially enroll in the tutorial program. A "Parent Consent and Waiver" form was also required of each participant to fill out and return to the specified site. After registration was complete, students were assigned to specific teachers who check attendance each day. Attendance records were submitted to and maintained by the Head teacher at the individual site. A copy of all daily attendance records for each tutorial site was available upon request.

Roles and Responsibilities of Staff and Head Teachers

The major role of the Head Teacher was to coordinate site activities, maintain records, and order and disseminate supplies. The teacher's role was to basically assess pupil needs, provide needed instruction, and maintain attendance and progress records. The aides and volunteers provided support services to the teachers and students.

Summary of CAL Impact

The Cultural Academic Life Skills component of the Louisiana Assistance Program has provided many excellent experiences and opportunities for academic growth and development. CAL has also served as a positive agent in the community which has promoted increased self-pride and cultural enhancement among citizens of the community. Additionally, this program has impacted students who have been involved as well as parents and teachers, both at the tutorial sites and in the public schools and administrators.

Specifically, the following comments were made by same of the teachers involved in the program. Valerie Ludley, who once taught first grade at Simsboro School said, "I can give the individual attention that I cannot give at school with 21 other students around." Dorothy Rodgers, a retired school teacher with 26 years of service in the Lincoln Parish schools, sees the students gaining confidence.

Last and most importantly the students viewed the tutorial program as "wonderful", "great", "fantastic," "a challenge," just to share a few of their expressions. One student wrote a poem which summarized his feelings. The poem was presented at one of the culminating enrichment programs presented on June 29, 1995:

CAL '95

CAL' 95 has been lots of fun,
There's no other program just like this one.
We had reading, math, and fun games, too.
That made learning great for me and for you.

Great Afro-Americans make our culture bright
We talked about many who have made things right.
Dr. King, Jesse Jackson, and others, too
worked hard to make their dreams come true.

Now we in CAL must find a way.
to better our future every day.
It takes pride and vision and determination
to stand up and be counted in this nation.

We learned about manners and attitude
that surely will heighten our altitude.
We enjoyed the food and also the art and
even the picnic at Charles P. Adams Park.

C stands for Culture, We all agree
A is for Academics ... That's important, you see;
L is for Life Skills that we all Need;
Put the Letters together and they spell succeed.

The time has come for CAL programs to end,
But we have a great big message to send...
"Thanks, Representative Wilkerson and Our Teachers, Too
From all CAL Kids to each of You!!!"

CHAPTER 22

INTEGRATING INSTRUCTIONAL TECHNOLOGY INTO UNDERGRADUATE TEACHER PREPARATION CURRICULUM AND GRADUATE SCHOOL PROGRAMS

Claude Perkins, Ph.D., Dean
School of Education
Albany State University

Burel Block, Ph.D., Program Coordinator
Administration and Supervision
Albany State University

Alice Duhon-Ross, Ph.D., Assistant Professor
School Counseling
Albany State University

This chapter examines how instructional technology is used as a delivery system for students enrolled in the undergraduate teacher preparation programs and graduate programs in the College of Education at Albany State University in Albany, Georgia.

Instructional Technology in the Undergraduate Program

In the Curriculum and Instruction department at Albany State University College of Education, students enrolled in the teacher education program are required to complete a computer course as a prerequisite for admission to the teacher education program. The course entitled *EDU 207: Computers for Teachers* was designed to help pre-service teachers to use computer technology to increase the efficiency and effectiveness of the educational process. Administrators and faculty in the C & I recognized that the classroom teachers were the most important element in computer assisted instruction. Properly trained teachers who have control over the computer assisted instruction can provide their students with an added dimension to learning. In the end, it is the classroom teachers' creativity, enthusiasm, and professional competence that will transform instruction into exemplary student achievement. Thus it becomes essential for students to have computer skills in order to successfully complete their teacher preparation program. Students enrolled in the computers for teacher course were instructed and participated in four stages of teacher involvement:

Basic Level:

At this level, the students were expected to understand the relationship of organizing and delivering instruction. Automatically this function is essential. Pre- service teachers may be expect to monitor student progress and make changes in prescribing instructional levels in response to performance reports. As they acquire the skills in data storage and retrieval, as well as data integration.

Application Level:

In the application level, the instructor continues to expect students to carry the major work load of reorganizing and delivering instruction. In addition, the Pre-service teacher is expected to have greater involvement in monitoring student progress and making adaptive placement in response to performance.

Connection Level:

In the connection level, students are expected to carry out the same functions as with the basic and application levels, but exercises greater control over the scope and sequence of activities. The Pre-service teacher will be able to edit activity sequences and integrate the use of multiple software programs to meet local curriculum requirements. (Merging of courseware with classroom programs.)

Extend Level:

At the extended level, students are expected to take full ownership and control over the computer delivery system. Students will be able to customize the courseware to local needs, integrate multiple software programs, test at any point on specified instructional outcomes, schedule and assign prospective students to meet local requirements such as; branching of courseware, integrate third party activities, complex scheduling, customize reporting or student performance. The computers for teachers courses are held in one of four computer labs with state of the art microcomputers, hypermedia software applications, CD-ROMs, LDC panels, graphic scanners, and a host of other computer peripherals.

Instructional Technology in the Graduate School

How is instructional technology used as a delivery system for graduate programs? What are the possibilities for using instructional technology in graduate program? These two questions will be addressed in this chapter.

212

Instructional technology allows instructors new venues for delivering instruction to graduate students.

In the leadership program at Albany State University enrolls many students who are full-time teachers. Some may drive as far as 100 miles to take a graduate class from 5:40 to 10:00 p.m. Many are coaches who do not have the time to take courses during basketball season or during football season. Some are interested in adding a certification in leadership, or attaining the Education Specialist Degree or the Doctor of Education in leadership.

Most graduate classes were offered at night after working hours so that professional educator could enroll in graduate school. With the advent of the Internet, closed circuit television, and the desktop computer, new alternatives to scheduling of classes and presentation of instruction have arrived.

The Leadership Program at Albany State University offers two courses that utilize the Internet to deliver instruction to graduate students. The first to go on-line was EAS 568 Field Experience in Educational Administration and Supervision. The second is EAS 570 School Business Management. The field experience course requires a graduate to spend 100 hours shadowing a school administrator who is a full-time employee of a school. The school administrator serves as a mentor and advisor for the student intern. The intern must log 100 clock hours in one of the twelve area as outlined in the EAS Field Experience Manual (see http://fld94.alsnet.peachnet.edu/bblock). Weekly logs are e-mailed to the program coordinator or the data are sent via the Microsoft Front Page form that is a part of the web page for the leadership program. Logs are also accepted via fax.

The intern and the school administrator agree on at least four projects that are related to the day to day work of the school administrator's duties. As the student works on these projects, the time spent is logged and described on a diskette and e-mailed to the university program coordinator. The web page contains a notice page that itemizes the requirements of the course. The web page also has an application that can be downloaded. Upon downloading the intern discusses the 4 or 5 projects that will be targeted with the school administrator. After agreeing on the planned projects the university instructor meets with the intern and the school administrator.

The intern completes the pre-assessment instrument, which is also downloaded from the web. The pre-assessment instrument contains 12 general areas of educational administration that are addressed in the course. These 12 areas are explained in detail in the EAS manual, which is also available on the web. The EAS manual contains examples of projects and explanations regarding the course.

The school administrator must agree to perform an evaluation of the intern's work, which is used to help determine the intern's grade for the course. The evaluation instrument is available on the web and can be printed and utilized. Because many graduate students are strapped for time, EAS 570 School Business Management was designed so that the lectures, reports, and discussions took place over a three-day weekend. Nine sessions on Friday, Saturday, and Sunday are used. There are three sessions on each day. The first session runs from 8 a.m. to 12 p.m. The second session runs from 1 p.m. to 5 p.m. The third session runs from 6 p. m. to 10 p.m. The final examination is given the following Saturday from 9 a.m. to 12 p.m.

The course syllabus and calendar are posted of the leadership web page. Nine lectures are posted on the web along with relevant research topics for each lecture. Nine lectures will be presented using Microsoft Power Point slide presentations. The sessions regarding budgets and budget controls will be presented in the computer lab with Microsoft Excel. Proposed budgets and Students are instructed to do all reading and research prior to the three-day weekend. Research topics are assigned via e-mail and the telephone so that there will be few duplications of topics. As students sign-up for research topics their names and topics will be logged.

The professor prepares part of the lecture at home and e-mails it to his office where he finishes the preparation or completes part of it and e-mails it back home for more work at night. After the lecture is completed it is e-mailed to work where it is downloaded to a lab top computer from which it is delivered via closed circuit television to three different locations simultaneously. The lecture is delivered in color, animation, and sound effects.

Brief program descriptions, tentative class schedules, and course offerings are available on the leadership web page. The instructor's e-mail address, telephone, and fax numbers are posted on the web. The preceding discussion has covered the first question: How is instructional technology used as a delivery system for graduate programs? The possibilities include tests given and corrected with the form configuration of Microsoft's Front Page. Research topic and the researcher's name could be submitted directly to the professor through a form on the web. Power Point presentations, lecture notes, books, programs of study, and course catalogues could all be placed on the Internet to facilitate communication with graduate students.

The use of the Internet reduces the amount of driving time for both professors and students. Power Point presentations can be delivered easily and effectively over closed circuit television as well as question and answer sessions. With the new and faster computer chips, we can expect to see more actual time video and audio, which will facilitate desktop instruction. Professors will sit in their offices and lecture to ten or fifteen students who will be at home taking notes on their own desktops. Fact is, professors could stay at home and lecture after dinner over their own desktop computers. Exchange of research will be facilitated by e-mail. Students will collaborate on research projects by sharing files (and viruses) via e-mail and the Internet.

In summary, the Internet, closed circuit television, lab top computers, desktop computers, Microsoft Power Point, Microsoft Front Page, and Microsoft Excel are utilized to present both the school business management course and the field experience course in the Leadership Program at Albany State University. The future holds the marvelous possibility of desktop lecturing in full video color and sound with the flexibility of staying at home to do graduate studies.

References

http://fld94.alsnet.peachnet.edu/bblock

Lemay, L. (1997). Web Workshop, Microsoft Front Page 97. New York: Sams.net Publishing

Geisert, P. G., & Futrell, M. K. (1995). Teachers Computers and Curriculum. Boston: Allyn Bacon.

216

CHAPTER 23

IMMUNITY TO THE IMMACULATE PERCEPTION:
AN AESTHETIC EDUCATION APPROACH
TO THE DEVELOPMENT OF CRITICAL THINKING

Nanthalia W. McJamerson, Ph.D.
Associate Professor
Department of Teacher Education
College of Education
Grambling State University
Grambling, LA

Jimmy McJamerson, M.A. +68
Assistant Professor
Department of History and Geography
College of Liberal Arts
Grambling State University
Grambling, LA

This chapter outlines the rationale for the implementation of an interdisciplinary aesthetic education curriculum as an effort to increase the development of critical thinking. Emphasis is placed on forces which support and oppose critical thinking in school-- forces within teachers and forces upon teachers in the schooling context and in the broader society.

> If you can control a man's thinking, you do not have to worry about his actions When you determine what a man shall think, you do not have to concern yourself about what he will do. If you make a man feel that he is inferior, you do not have to compel him to accept an inferior status, for he will seek it himself. (Woodson, 1933, p. 84)

Schooling has come under harsh criticism in the past decades, for failing to produce critical thinkers. The National Assessment of Educational Progress (NEP) personnel reported that "Johnny and Janey" can finally read, but they cannot think. Some educators and assessment agencies are arguing that even

217

though functionally literate, many students are not literate enough to seize the power of the curriculum content for changing the course of their destiny. Several critics contend that schools are producers of "nervous right-answer givers" and are places which enslave rather than free minds. This chapter focuses on one schooling problem which underlies those above: the lack of teaching for critical thinking.

This is an inquiry into the ways in which an approach to teaching for critical thinking was implemented when taken into the conventional schooling process of an elementary school. The chapter focuses upon two teachers who were assigned the task of implementing the critical teaching embodied within an aesthetic education curriculum project. Based upon observation and interview data, an investigation was made of their behavior patterns and the influences upon those patterns over the two-year span of the Project.

The purpose of this chapter is to increase our understanding of the development of critical thinking. It addresses more than the teaching of critical thinking skills and particular sets of teaching techniques. Rather, the chapter is based upon schooling behavior that instructs and inspires spires students to question and transform their social realities. It is an investigation of ways that people are empowered or denied empowerment to determine the course of their own lives through the stifling versus development of critical thinking in school. Ira Shor (1980) explains:

> A pedagogy which empowers students to intervene in the making of
> history is more than a literacy campaign. Critical education prepares
> students to be their own agents for social change, their own creators of
> democratic culture . . . Thus, inferences to critical thought must be
> conceived as social and pervasive, not as personal problems or as isolated
> pedagogical ones... A population richly critical and creative would be a
> risk to hierarchy and exploitation. Critical learning aids people in knowing
> what holds them back; it encourages them to envision a social order which
> supports their full humanity. (p.48)

Furthermore, the chapter does not purport to add another negative description of anti-critical or oppressive schooling experiences but rather to provide insight about alternative practices that can move toward democracy and social justice.

The research questions which guided the chapter were:

1. What are the variations in the schooling behavior of two teachers in implementing the critical thinking teaching approach embodied within an aesthetic education curriculum?

2. What influence did their social experiences, circumstances in the school setting and societal trends have upon the variation in their implementation of this critical thinking teaching approach?

The definition of schooling as used in this chapter is the acts of teachers and other authorities to arrange the environment and influence the lives of children, in the present and in their becoming adults" (Berlak and Berlak, 1975, p. 11). This chapter is an investigation of those acts as they relate to the development of critical thinking. Teaching for the development of critical thinking is defined in this chapter as a three-component approach: (1) Opportunity for Student Control-a predominance of shared control between teachers and students (2) Revelation of Human Action-the presentation of curriculum content as the product of human action and (3) School Content/Personal Life Connection-an emphasis on student ownership of subject matter as instruments for evaluating and transforming their lives.

Aesthetic education promised this type of emancipatory, critical teaching approach and thus it was the area that was studied. I became involved in the Aesthetic Education Project in 1980, while working with Advocates of New Ways of Schooling (ANEWA) one of several federally funded projects designed to solve sate of the nation's educational problems. This (ANEWA) project purported to develop critical thinking and literacy through its approach to teaching the arts. I followed the curriculum into Iman School, a predominantly Black, urban elementary school located in the South. This chapter was based upon observation and interview data collected during periodic site visits over the two-year span of the Project.

I entered Iman School in a dual role: as an evaluator (participant observer) for (ANEWA) and as a critical social scientist for the present study. The task for (ANEWA) was to evaluate the training, implementation and effects of the Project's art components. However, my task as the critical social scientist was to look "deeper" and portray the schooling behavior of the participants in order to illuminate complexities of behavior and its influences as they related to carrying out the critical teaching approach embodied in aesthetic education. The Berlaks' dilemma language provided the means for making such an inquiry. Their Dilemma Language of Schooling is an interpretive framework grounded in

George Herbert Mead's dialectical view of human thought and behavior. This analytical language consists of sixteen dilemmas as a way of describing the schooling acts of teachers. Through analysis of teachers' dominant and exceptional patterns of resolution to the dilemmas, the dilemma framework provides a means of not only describing the schooling process but also of analyzing the origins and consequences of schooling behavior.

Using the Berlaks' dilemma language, I portrayed and analyzed what happened to the teaching of critical thinking in the "real world" of an elementary school. The chapter illuminated the complexity and nuance with which two teachers used the same curriculum and created notably different teaching patterns relative to instructing and encouraging critical thinking. The chapter revealed how and why one teacher maintained a traditional approach to teaching, over the too-year span, while the other teacher converted to a more critical teaching approach. In addition, an exploration was made of the influences upon their behavior patterns, influences in their social experiences, in the school setting and in societal traditions and trends.

By clarifying the struggle involved in teaching for critical thinking, the chapter contributes insight necessary for informed action that can address the complex networks of both the problems for and possibilities of teaching for critical thinking. Such awareness can lead to the development of strategies for supporting those actions and forces that support critical teaching. Furthermore, the awareness of opposing actions and forces can lead to counteraction or negating strategies. Consequently, the increase of teaching for critical thinking could have students toward human emancipation

This chapter addresses the concern that schools are failing to engage students in schooling experiences that will enable them to critically examine and transform their lives. This is not a new problem; educators have wrestled with the critical thinking issue in several versions for many years. Thus it is important that I clarify the particular teaching approach for developing critical thinking that is used in this chapter.

The definition of critical thinking itself most often cited is that of Robert Ennis (1962): the reasonable assessment of statements. From this perspective, critical thinking refers primarily to teaching students "how to analyze and develop reading and writing assignments from the perspective of formal, logical patterns of consistency (Giroux, 1978, p.298). There have been numerous studies conducted in efforts to teach those skills. Bryce Hudgins (1977) notes many studies of efforts to teach for critical thinking development, and he notes H. P. Fawcett's two-year project in teaching geometry to high school students as one of the earliest and most comprehensive' of such studies. Fawcett's work resulted in improvement in students' critical thinking skills in geometry, in nonmathematical activities and outside the classroom (pp. 190-192). Another example of successfully teaching critical thinking was the work of Edward Glaser (1941). His work has been cited by Hudgins (1977), Shane and Walden (1978) and others as a classic experiment. The results of the investigation indicated that the students who were taught by methods dealing with concepts of critical thinking made significantly greater gains on the Watson-Glaser Tests of Critical Thinking than did the students who studied the regular subject content (Shane and Walden, 1978, p. 19). Also, there is a current resurgence of interest in programs to teach for critical thinking skills.

The accusations that schools are not producing critical thinkers pertain to the stance that more is involved in critical thinking than particular sets of skills. Entangled in critical thinking development are issues of empowerment, of will and capacity to judge and transform the world, of social reproduction and social change. Teaching approaches for developing this type of critical thinking require the restructuring or transformation of traditional and technocratic teaching approaches. What follows is a review of the works of three persons in the area of critical pedagogy: Paulo Freire (1970, 1973), Ira Shor (1980) and Henry Giroux (1978, 1980). From the synthesis of their work, an approach to teaching for critical thinking is formed for use in this chapter. This approach is embedded in the aesthetic education curriculum upon which the chapter is based. Thus the second section of the chapter reviews some of the literature which illuminates aesthetic education as a form of a critical thinking teaching approach.

Critical Consciousness

Paulo Freire's (1973) literacy program is a well known approach to the development of critical thinking. Though his program resulted in exile for him, Freire designed; gned a program in which literacy and political awareness would evolve simultaneously-critical consciousness. The process of developing critical literacy for Freire constituted cultural action for freedom. From the beginning, Freire rejected a mechanistic literacy program. Instead, he opted for a literacy program in relation to "awakening of the participants' consciousness; introduction to democratization of culture; with men as its subjects rather than patient recipients" (Freire, 1973, p.43). Freire's program began with the conviction that the role of man was not only to be in the world, but to engage in relations with the world, through acts of creation and re-creation. This requires more than the use of particular teaching techniques for the acquisition of particular skills. Freire explains:

> To acquire literacy is more than to psychologically and mechanically dominate reading and writing techniques. It is to dominate these techniques in terms of consciousness; to understand what one reads and to write what one understands; it is to <u>communicate</u> graphically. Acquiring literacy does not involve memorizing sentences, words, or syllables-lifeless objects unconnected to an existential universe-but rather an attitude of creation and recreation, a self transformation producing a stance of intervention in one's context (p. 48).

There are four major features of Freire's program. First, teachers studied the world of students, using what was learned from students' lives and language as the content for teaching them literacy. Secondly, teachers used content based on the concept of culture. A distinction is made between the world of nature and the world of culture as the result of man's labor or his efforts to create and recreate. He perceived reading and writing as keys to the world of written communication. In short, the role of man was that of subject rather than object in the world and with the world (p.46).

Thirdly, the illiterate would begin a change in attitude, discovering himself to be a maker of the world of culture, by discovering that he, as well as the literate person, has a creative and re-creative impulse. They discover that culture is their peer's clay doll as well as the artist's sculpture; the popular song as well as lettered poetry-that culture is all human creation (p. 47). To introduce the concept of culture, first educators "broke down" the concept into its fundamental aspects. Then codified (represented visually) ten existential situations. Each representation contained several elements to be "decoded" by the group participants, with the help of the coordinator.

Finally, once perceiving a distinction between nature and culture and recognizing man's role in each, the coordinator presents situations focusing on or expanding other aspects of culture. The conclusion is a debate of the democratization of culture, which opens the perspective of acquiring literacy (p.48). Freire's method resulted in discussions which were critical, stimulating and highly motivating. The illiterate perceived, critically, that it is necessary to learn to read and write and prepares himself to become the agent of this learning.

Freire (1970) summarizes the method: ". . . the educator's role is fundamentally to enter into dialogue with the illiterate about concrete situations and simply offer him the instruments with which he can teach himself to read and write" (p.48). Shor (1980) describes the process as the arrangement of an "encounter between students and their human capacity to transform the world" (p. 126).

Critical Teaching and Everyday Life

Ira Shor has done theoretical and practical work in the area of teaching for critical thinking. He noted that Freire provided the framework within which he was able to enhance his critical teaching. He credited Freire with providing dialogue as the foundation for the learning process. He espoused that co-investigation of reality and systematization of daily knowledge are primary' vehicles for advancing language skills. According to Shor, the "conceptual inquiry" into reality is the final step in empowing students to think critically.

Shor (1980) designed conceptual exercises for the simultaneous development of reading, writing and critical thought. They involved three major steps. First, the requirement is observation, in which close scrutiny is exercised regarding the object, concept or issue under study and then a connection is made to students' native language and everyday experience. The second step is diagnosis. Diagnosis goes beyond description to analysis. This involves researching the problematic nature of the thing under observation-investigating the roots and consequences. The final step is reconstruction in which students are asked to redesign the thing under study so that the problem can be resolved-re-invented so that the future will not reproduce the present. The result of the process was that students participated in activities with a lively sense of what they were seeing, rejecting and rebuilding in their social lives.

Shor (1980) often asked students to practice the three-part method on classroom chairs, hamburgers and other aspects of their everyday reality. The "conceptual detectives in dialogue" were then asked to use the method on two things at hare, then on something in the neighborhood and finally on society. This historical consciousness stimulates students' imaginations for discovering alternatives to their social reality. The empowering result is that: "Students who gain the power to understand the transformations of society also gain the critical consciousness needed to invent their own transformations" (Shor, 1980, p. l66).

Critical thinking: More Than a thinking problem

Giroux (1978) identifies the type of teaching/learning process to which students are exposed as one pert of the problem of a lack of critical thinking. He labels the process as "the pedagogy of the immaculate perception" which involves (1) systematic exposure to selected material, presented as unquestionable and value free; (2) learning approaches which sanction dominant categories and stifle structural insight and (3) hierarchical classroom social relationships which produce students who are afraid or unable to think critically (p. 297).

Giroux (1978) notes, however, that pedagogy is not the source of critical thinking problems in North American can schools. He contends,

> ... it is too simple-minded a response to lay the blame exclusively on either
> teachers or students. Such a perspective ignores that the essence of
> schooling lies in particularly the institutions of work. Schools appear to
> have little to do with the Kantian notion that they should function to
> educate students for a "better future condition of the human race, that is for
> the idea of humanity" (Marcuse, 1972, 27). The real business of schools
> appears to be to socialize students into accepting and reproducing the
> existing society (p. 297).

Although pedagogy or teaching is not exclusively the problem, Giroux suggests that it can be a part of the solution to the development of critical thinkers if teachers can examine some of the assumptions behind their approaches to teaching. He begins the work toward developing a pedagogy of critical thinking with the definition of critical thinking and suggests a sociological framework for teaching it.

The major facets of this sociological view of teaching critical thinking are succinctly explained by Giroux (1978). He suggests that the basic assumptions underlying critical thinking should form the programmatic groundwork for creating critical thinking pedagogy. Those core assumptions are: (1) a relationship exists between theory and fact and (2) knowledge cannot be separated from human interests, norms and values. Related to the two assumptions about critical thinking is a procedural issue that centers around what Giroux (1978) calls the contextualization of information.

Students need to learn how to be able to move outside of their own frame of reference so that they can question the legitimacy of a given fact, concept, or issue. They also have to learn how to perceive the very essence of what they are examining by placing it critically within a system of relationships that give it meaning (p. 299)

Also related to the assumptions at the core of critical thinking is a second facet of critical thinking pedagogy, classroom social relations. Any approach to critical thinking, regardless of how progressive it might be, will vitiate its own possibilities if it operates out of a web of classroom social relationships that are authoritatively hierarchical and promote passivity, docility, and silence. Social relationships in the classroom that glorify the teacher as the expert, the dispenser of knowledge, end up crippling student imagination and creativity in addition, such approaches teach students more about the legitimacy of passivity than about the need to examine critically the lives they lead (Giroux, 1978, p. 300).

The fundamental practice of critical thinking pedagogy is having students go through the process of making the same kinds of choices every historian, artist, etc., makes, consequently, enabling students to judge knowledge for what it is: human attempts to explain reality or change reality. This is accomplished, Giroux believes, by guiding students "inside" a subject and having them think critically so that they may provide their own interpretations of the material.

Giroux presented a model of critical thinking pedagogy in the subject areas of history and writing. He suggested that a viable approach to an integrated pedagogy of writing and history would begin by developing a method by which students would be taught something about the nature of history. This could be done, according to Giroux, by showing students how to read history by first showing them how history is written. Basically, students would go through the process of making the same kinds of choices that every historian makes. Consequently, "students should be taught to judge any history for what it is--an author's attempt to explain the significance of what happened and why it happened" (Giroux, 1978).

Giroux (1980) elaborated his version of critical pedagogy which includes the following assumptions and practices. First, Giroux contends that the active nature of students' participation is stressed. Opportunities should be provided for students to produce and criticize classroom meanings. Secondly, students must be taught to think critically, to move beyond literal interpretations and fragmented modes of reasoning. Students should not be enslaved to the concrete fact versus

225

learning to move beyond viewing issues in isolation. Facts, concepts, issues and ideas must be seen within the network of connections that give them meaning. Students learn to look at the world holistically in order to understand the interconnections of the parts to each other. Thirdly, critical thinking pedagogy would enable students to appreciate their own biographies and systems of meaning. They should be given opportunities to speak with their own voices; to authenticate their own experiences. The significance here is that when the will to act is deadened, questions about critical thinking become empty chatter. Finally, according to Giroux (1980), students must not only clarify values but also must comprehend the source of their own beliefs and actions. Because awareness can change possibilities, students must learn how values are embedded in the texture of human life; how values are transmitted and what interests they support regarding the quality of human existence.

Based on the work of Freire, Shor and Giroux, three major components of a teaching approach for developing critical thinking can be delineated. The first component is the provision of opportunities for student control or input. The second component is the revelation of human action in subject matter rather than mystification. Finally, a connection must be made between school content and students' personal lives.

Aesthetic Education as an Approach to Teaching Critical Thinking

Those who have had artistic/aesthetic training are given credit for having great power for penetrating the subtleties and mysteries of life. Many people are awed by their perception and by their creative and critical expression. In some countries artists are persecuted because of their perceptual and critical powers. In this section, I will review some of the literature to show that much of the clamor over aesthetic education concerns the connection between aesthetic experience and critical thinking. That is, aesthetic education can contribute to the critical examination and transformation of our lives.

The conceptual connection between aesthetic education and critical thinking is, in part, within the relationship between art and science. Both the "scientific spirit and aesthetic sensitivity" are considered as more than parts of the sane method but rather as substance of the sane ethic, according to Dewey (1916):

> The function which science has to perform in the curriculum is that which it has performed for the race: emancipation from local and temporary

incidents of experience, and the opening of intellectual visits. Thus ultimately and philosophically science is the organ of general social progress. . . The moral of art itself is to remove prejudice, do away with the scales that keep the eye from seeing, tear away veils due to wont or custom, perfect the power to perceive. (p.229)

There are pedagogical connections between critical thinking and aesthetic education. An essential part of aesthetic education is the unleashing of imagination and critique. Also, students have an opportunity to investigate, analyze, express, respond, re-conceive, re-create from various perspectives, in part, as they take on varied roles of creator, implementor, audience, critic (Smith, 1977). Eisner (1978) discusses the operational connection between aesthetic education and critical thinking development:

That is that children learn when they paint, draw, or make three-dimensional images? . . . They can create images altering symbols... which can lead to consciousness then communication... processes of image-making require the making of judgments (not rule-seeking, like spelling). The locus of evaluation moves from external to internal... They learn that images can be related to other images to form a whole decentrate perception... They learn to create illusion and to form images that are visually persuasive. This skill increases transforming powers... plays a role in consciousness... and the development of confidence and competence... Reflection is invited.

What children eventually learn is a way of looking at life.

The development of critical thinking as instrumental in trans-forming our social reality involves moral and political components. Newman (1978) delineates what it is about aesthetic education that fosters the moral aspect of critical thinking.

1. There is moral import in the nonstereotypic quality of this mode of cognition. Aesthetic education deals with acute, exciting perception of individuals, not generalities, which should offset our tendencies to be slaves to stereotypes and clichés.

2. Corollary to nonstereotyping and authenticity is the inclination to embrace varying perspectives, look at phenomena from fresh vantage points-to cast off traditional paradigms.

227

3. The "fittingness" aspect of AE requires weighing the appropriateness of alternative courses of action in accordance with how they fit relevant situational variables.

4. Empathy, regarding others identical to ones elf, demands sympathetic appreciation of appropriate scientific modes of inquiry and sensitive consideration of myriad data from scientific research. Rationality is insufficient.

In summary, Newman argues that aesthetic education should become a regular part of schooling because of the moral/social effects on personality. Another connection between critical thinking and aesthetic education is the identical position the two areas represent concerning the social reproduction vs. social change dilemma. Critical thinking or critical examination and transformation of reality "falls" on the side of social change. Addressing the pedagogical and curriculum question concerning the role of schooling in social change involves educational experiences, created or nurtured by teachers, which are "capable of altering the ways in which a person views the world" (Berlak, 1977, p. 36). Eisner (1978) and others in the aesthetic field agree that such experiences are provided in aesthetic education.

Beyer (1979) makes a case for the connection between critical thinking and aesthetic education at a different level: the role of aesthetic education in social reproduction and change. He acknowledges that such an analysis involves many complex philosophical issues, and could easily become the subject of one's life work, but he argues that, it is in the connection between aesthetic meanings and ethical deliberation eration and conduct that aesthetic value most significantly resides. According to Beyer, when an art work affects our thoughts and feelings in a profound and significant way, it also affects the way we feel about and think through the issues raised or the subject matter presented in the work of art. The aesthetic participant may then be led to think and act differently. He clarifies:

Art and the aesthetic thus have the power to make us see our world differently, to view our individual and collective situations from a new perspective and change how we will respond to the events in our lives. When a work of art makes us see some object, person, or event in a new way, to consider it from a fresh perspective, it can inform and reform our perception of that object or event... Aesthetic forms can, in short, move the viewer to enlightened social action (Beyer, p. 5).

Beyer further contends that the sort of potential value for the aesthetic experience he posited above is rarely manifested within the educational establishment of this country. He suggests a reason for the void: "The political dimension inherent in these aesthetic experiences, their ability to make us see ourselves and our relation to others in new ways, that accounts for the lack of such aesthetic experience within schools." He argues that there is a basic, fundamental disharmony between such a political or "emancipatory" aspect of aesthetic forms and the functions of schooling: "The ideological function of educational institutions militates against taking aesthetic forms seriously in the way characterized above." (p.5) Beyer explains:

In that aesthetic value is connected to ethical deliberation and enlightened social action, aesthetic experience contains a political element, in affecting how we view, feel about, and value our world. That is, the role of schooling as an agent of social reproduction may work against the emancipatory component of aesthetic forms. (p. 6)

The struggle continues. When the school site was revisited a decade after implementation the principal and one teacher were attempting to keep the aesthetic education alive by integrating activities into the faculty lesson plans. The better the contradictory forces upon this type of pedagogy, the greater our chances of success.

References

Berlak A., & Berlak, H. (1981). The dilemmas of schooling. London: Methuen.

Beyer, L. E. (1979). Schools, aesthetic forms, and social reproduction. Madison: University of Wisconsin. (Draft)

Dewey, J. (1916). Democracy and education. New York: Free Press.

Eisner, E. (1976, February). Reading and the creation of meaning. Paper read as keynote address to the Claremont Reading Conference, February, 1976, Claremont, CA, 1976.

Ennis, R. H. (1956). Critical thinking: More on its motivation. Progressive Education, 75-84.

Freire, P. (1973). Pedagogy of the oppressed. New York: Seabury.

Giroux, H. A. (1978). Writing and critical thinking in the social studies. Curriculum Inquiry, 8(1), 291-310.

Glaser, B. and A. Strauss, A. (1967). The discovery of grounded theory: Strategies for qualitative research. Chicago: Aldine.

Henry, J. Golden rule days: American schoolrooms. Culture against man. New York: Vintage.

Holt, J. (1964). How children fail. New York: Dell.

Hudgins, B. B. (1977). Learning and thinking: A primer for teachers. Itasca, Ill.: F. E. Peacock.

Newman, A. (1980). Aesthetic sensitizing and moral education." Journal of Aesthetic Education, 93-101.

Paul, R. (1993). Critical thinking: How to prepare students for a rapidly changing world. Santa Rosa, CA: Foundations for Critical Thinking.

Paul, R., Binker, A. J. A., & others. (1990). Critical thinking handbook: 4th-6th grades. A guide for remodeling lesson plans in language arts, social studies, & science (2nd ed.). Santa Rosa, CA: Foundation for Critical Thinking.

Shor, I. (1980). Critical Teaching and Everyday Life. Boston: South End Press.

Shor, I. (1992). Empowering education: Critical teaching for social change. Chicago: University of Chicago Press.

Smith, L. M., & Geoffrey, W. (1968). The complexities of an urban classroom. New York: Holt, Rinehart, and Winston.

Wirth, A. (1983). Productive work in the industry and schools: Becoming persons again. New York: University Press of America.

Table 3
Summary of Findings on Dilemmas of Critical Teaching

	Support for Critical Teaching	Opposition to Critical Teaching
Behavior Patterns	Opportunity for student control Mrs. F: Dominant Mode Mrs. R: Exceptional Mode	Lack of Student Input and Expression Mrs. F: Exceptional Mode Mrs. R: Dominant Mode
	Revelation of Human Action Mrs. F: Exceptional Mode Mrs. R: Exceptional Mode	Treatment of Content as Given "Truths" Mrs. F: Dominant Mode Mrs. R: Dominant Mode
	Connection of School Content to Personal Life Mrs. F: Dominant Mode Mrs. R: Exceptional Mode	Mastery of Content for Evaluation Mrs. F: Exceptional Mode Mrs. R: Dominant Mode
Influences Upon Behavior	From Past Experiences • As a student, recalled an unfulfilled desire for personal expression in the classroom • Developed a view of childhood as a time for enjoyment	From Past Experiences • As a student, exposed to teacher-controlled activity • As student and teacher, emphasis on "silence" via proper conduct and order • Teacher training emphasized textbooks, manuals and recitation • As student and teacher, school portrayed as "serious business"– preparation for the future
	From Contemporary Setting • Encouragement by principal • ANEWA training workshops • ANEWA curriculum material • Positive effects upon students	From Contemporary Setting • Emphasis on standardized tests superseded other student outcomes • Stronghold of functional literacy goals (of teachers and district administration)– riveted to the "basics" • Restricted resources for aesthetic education
	From the Societal Level • No support noted	From the Societal Level • High test score trend • Value of "following the rules" (both indices of future opportunities and success)

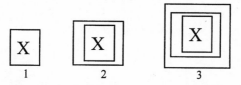

1.   X in the square is the theme or object under problematic study.

2.   The larger square represents X in its immediate social setting. How does X relate to other aspects of social life? What are the human consequences of X? For example, a contextual analysis of the car. How do cars get made and sold? Why do cars look like they do? What are all the things people use cars for?

3.   The next large square represents the global relations of X. Does it exist in France, China? Does our use of cars affect life elsewhere on the planet? Why do other countries build them and sell them here? Who organizes this kind of system?

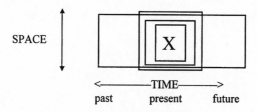

4.   The new rectangle moves backwards and forwards in time. This new direction seeks to know how each student's life has been involved recently with X. Further, it probes the immediate future vís a vís X. The car example: when was the specific vehicle you use built? In terms of cars, what social changes will be affecting their use in the next few years?

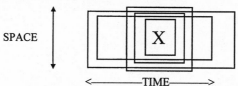

5.   The larger rectangle is the long-range time span of X. When did it first enter human history? Has it changed since then? Who brought it into being and why? *How could X look if it were reconstructed along different ideas? What changes are needed in it?*

Figure 1
Shor's Conceptual Paradigm

Chapter 24
Empowering the At-Risk Reader: Teaching Strategies

Mary M. Addison, Ed.D.
Margaret N. Stroud, Ed.D
Dolores A. Westmoreland Ed.D.
Houston Independent School District
Houston, TX

> *Have you ever rightly considered what the mere ability to read means?*
> *That it is the key which admits us to the whole world of thought and*
> *fancy and imagination. That it enables us to see with the keenest eyes,*
> *hear with the finest ears, and listen to the sweetest voices of all time?*
> *James Russell Lowell, Democracy and other Addresses: Books and Libraries.*
> *Quoted in The Home Book of American Quotations (1986, p. 337).*

The above quotation from the poet, James Russell Lowell, should be the foundation of the inspirational mantra for all educators.   "Education has no meaning for students who have not acquired the ability to read. What good is it to ask a student to define a given word in the context of a specific paragraph if he cannot pronounce the word? Similarly, how can the student decide upon the *main idea* of a standardized testing selection if he cannot read the material for meaning?

Much of the responsibility for empowering students with reading abilities has been placed at the feet of elementary teachers by a public which demands that students acquire reading skills by grade three. In the "good old days" elementary teachers were presented reading candidates whose parents had spent quality time with their offspring engaging in reading preparation activities Similarly, middle and high school students were encouraged to read for pleasure by having many magazines and books available in the home or being taken to the library to obtain recreational reading materials. Unfortunately, in today's hectic society, many students are at-risk because they do not have the parental guidance nor the reading materials provided to encourage this skill. Recalling Maslow's hierarchy, when a parent is struggling to provide the income for necessities such as food and shelter, magazine subscriptions, encyclopedia purchases, and time for recreational reading with one's children does not receive much merit. Subsequently, students are arriving in all grade-level classrooms lacking the motivation and preparation to be successful readers. It becomes the responsibility of the classroom teacher and administrators to identify teaching strategies which will insure reading success in any classroom environment.

The information presented in this chapter should prove helpful to teachers of students on any grade level (K- 12) and in any educational environment (Regular education, Limited English proficiency, special education resource, special education inclusion, etc.) who are considered at-risk because they have not accumulated the necessary reading skills to allow them to read for edification and education.

Stages in Reading Development

It would be a safe assumption to declare that the majority of elementary and secondary certified teachers have not bad a plethora of reading methodology courses listed on their college transcripts; therefore a review of the sequential developmental stages to acquiring reading proficiency would be helpful.

1. *Phonemic Awareness*

When children are born, their first association with language is external through speech They begin to bear words and soon learn to associate the sound of different words with specific actions---"No", "Stop", "Eat", etc. As they begin kindergarten, they are shown that each word heard can be divided into smaller individual sounds (phonemes) and can pronounce a written word by blending the spoken sounds into a word. The students are honing their auditory and listening skills when they begin to identify the sounds of the phonemes. The goal of this activity is not to memorize and recite tedious rules governing letter-sound relationships, but to recognize the correspondence between letters and their sounds through repetitive practice.

When students learn to sound out words, it provides them a catalyst for independently identifying words in a passage which are unknown to them. Moreover by sounding out a word, the students attention is directed to the identity and order of the letters in the word. By reading decodable stories, students are given an opportunity to practice the letter and sound relationships introduced. Research has demonstrated that the child who realizes that all spoken words can be phonetically pronounced by dividing them into syllables and phonemes is well on his way to reading achievement and fluency.

2.   Print awareness

Through the magic of advertising, children can recognize a variety of environmental print that they encounter daily through exposure from television repeated readings of the same story book, business establishment signs, etc. Parents have found the primary books of such children's authors as Dr. Seuss excellent tools for developing word awareness because of the colorful and unique graphics which accompany the written word. Children think that they are "reading" because the visual cues provide the stimulus for word. recognition. Studies have shown when certain words which are recognized by children under the age of five because of being a specific color, were reprinted in another color, the children did not recognize them. Reading books to children allows them to observe the arrangement for reading (i.e. left to right)

3.   Alphabetic awareness

In kindergarten, the students have an opportunity to learn the twenty-six building blocks of the written language and how they can be intentionally combined to form spoken words. Learning the alphabet is sometimes a difficult process for students and quite frustrating for their parents.   Parents cannot understand how their child who can tell them the nightly television programming order flawlessly will fail to master the twenty-six single letters in the proper order or individually. One reason is because the letters are abstract and unless they are associated with a concrete object (i.e. "A is for Apple") are difficult to retain. Additionally, research has shown that letters are not learned holistically but as a shape which is defined by its horizontal, vertical or diagonal line segments as well as its arcs. Because of this, many readers who fail to recognize the orientation of a given letter were pronounced neurologically challenged when in fact they just needed additional practice on letter shapes. Children must learn to recognize both upper and lower rase forms of the printed alphabet as well as the two cases in cursive.

Children who demonstrate an adroitness for letter recognition will experience an early success with reading because they will interested in the sound of the letter and how it can be combined with others to spell words. Likewise, this recognition has been shown to be associated with the child's ability to recall the forms of written words and the inclination to view the printed word as a sequence of ordered letters rather than a single group.

Teachers need to correlate the sound of the alphabet letter with its symbol and encourage reading of stories which reinforce the letters with its sound. The more that students can apply what they have learned through activities, the greater will be their retention level.

4. Orthographic Awareness

Now that the student has learned his alphabet and how to pronounce the letters, he needs to associate this information with the written words on the page. When a student is reading, his eyes observe the pattern of letters on the page and will associate the spelling with something in his memory which allows him to recognize the word. If there is no such association in his memory for a given word, his phonemic ability will enable him to sound out the word and identify it's meaning.

Written practice in spelling the words learned through reading will allow eye to hand coordination for the student and will result in better writing skills. Also learning to spell will reinforce a student's knowledge regarding. common letter sequences and may assist in awareness of word parts. As the students listen to their teacher pronounce the words to be spelled, they are improving their listening comprehension.

Initially the students are learning to spell the vocabulary words in the given reading lessons. Later, they will be introduced to such intricate spellings as homonyms and irregular letter pairings.

5. Reading Comprehension

When John Locke (17O7, p.20) stated, "Reading furnishes the mind only with materials of knowledge: it is thinking that makes what we read ours," he was certainly referring to the next reading developmental stage reading comprehension. it does little good for students to phonetically decode all of the words in a passage if they have little understanding of their meaning. The ultimate goal of reading is comprehension.

The student must be an active participant in the reading process to achieve comprehension. To achieve reading comprehension, the reader must be adroit in recognizing context clues of unfamiliar words in the passage. A context clue will not predict the precise meaning of a word but when this word is encountered again in another passage the reader will recall what was learned from the previous context encounter and will apply it to the current context encounter. The more times that a reader is exposed to a given word in various reading contexts, the better the definition is refined for his memory. A prolific reader could be expected to have a larger vocabulary and higher comprehension understanding because of the greater exposure to different words. Students should be encouraged to read often for pleasure to increase their comprehension skills because, as the English poet Joseph Addison, "Reading is to the mind what exercise is to the body" (Addison, 1992, p. 291)

Since, realistically, it is known that all students do not "flock to the library" to check out reading materials, teachers must utilize other methods for increasing comprehension. One such technique is planned vocabulary instruction. This would include giving students a list of words to research in the dictionary to improve their word knowledge and increase reading comprehension. As has been demonstrated in high schools, students who have an organized vocabulary list to research weekly have raised their verbal SAT and ACT scores.

Another method for increasing reading comprehension through word identification is the teaching of prefixes suffixes and roots. Teaching students the morphological derivation of words will increase their ability to discern the meanings of unfamiliar words with similar derivatives. Again this is a powerful tool for the high school student to have when entering the SAT examination room.

6.   *Reading Practice*

Henry David Thoreau (1986, p. 337) stated in his *Walden* writings, "To read well is a noble exercise." For students to comply with Thoreau's opinion, they must improve their reading skills by reading frequently and expansively. Like any other skill which must be refined, "practice does make perfect".

Reading is the principal avenue for students to improve their fluency, comprehension, vocabulary, and general knowledge. As Thomas D'Evelyn (1986, p. 64) so succinctly opined, "Man is what he reads." It is the responsibility of educators to provide opportunities for student's to "read to succeed".

Preparation Considerations for Formal Instruction

Just as the contractor would not consider erecting. a twenty-story building without an adequate foundation, teachers must give some consideration to the preparatory foundation of their future readers and plan accordingly prior to the commencement of formal reading instruction. Some salient suggestions for consideration are among these:

1. *Read aloud to the students.* Research has shown that this is the primary activity which teachers may employ to build skills and knowledge required for future reading. Children whose teachers regularly read aloud to them develop excellent listening skills and long attention spans.

2. *Students learn with adult interaction.* When students interact with adults, they learn faster. Just handing students a book or a worksheet and telling them to complete the assignment is never as effective as working with them.

3. *Students may express themselves better orally.* This has been found to be true of students for whom English is not their primary language. When Hispanic students take Spanish in high school, it is often thought that they would be exemplary students. They may understand the oral presentation but have difficulty with the written material. The same is true of elementary students who can converse well but do not understand that sentences are composed of many words.

4. *Preschool children's first acquaintance with the alphabet is through song.* Children have learned the alphabet through rote singing of the *Alphabet Song.* They are unable to identify the alphabet by shapes or sounds until later when taught at school.

5. Environmental print recognition does not increase reading proficiency. Students' recognition of environmental print does not contribute to reading proficiency unless they have learned about their individual letters previously.

6. Printing by young children should be encouraged. This activity has been shown to improve letter recogition and independent writing.

Initiation of Reading

Teachers' beginning a reading program in their classrooms should review the following research findings (Adams, 1990):

1. *Instructional program assignment is not productive.* Studies have shown that assigning students to an instructional program based upon their dominant modality or learning style does not appear to improve the effectiveness of their instruction,

2. *Programs should strive for a balanced approach.* Just as teachers know that the lecture method is not always the most conducive to learning so the teacher of reading should strive to have a variety of activities for the learners and not just all phonics or all reading. Recall that if activities which reinforce the process are meaningful to the students they will retain the information.

3. *Correlate coding instruction with reading exercises.* Using an approach which correlates the reading exercises in the text with the coding information being presented will assist both low-readiness and more astute students. Secondary students must see relevancy to what they are being required to do or they will not cooperate nor learn.

4. *Choose reading texts carefully.* The stories which are being read have been shown to influence the students reading abilities; therefore, select a text which has a large proportion of decodable words, good syntax, vocabulary and encourages higher order thinking skills. Such a choice will encourage independent reading and word recognition growth.

5. *Spelling reinforces phonetics.* The spelling exercises reinforce the phonetic sounds being presented and allow the student eye to hand coordination and improves auditory skills as he writes out the sounds he hears.

6. *Writing deepens comprehension.* Students who are given writing assignments to complete independently obtain a better apreciation for the information being presented in their reading texts and acquire a deeper comprehension.

Phonetic Observations

For the beginning elementary instructor or the secondary teacher who are not proficient in phonics the following observations should prove beneficial (Adams, 1990);

1. *Phonics assists spelling.* By sounding out their words, students become better spellers because their attention is directed towards the sounds of the word's letters and syllables.

2. *Readers should relate to phonics.* Application of a principle is the best way to retain it, thus, reading texts should have a correspondence with the specific phonics lesson being presented.

3. *Letter recognition is important.* Letter recognition skills are imperative to word recognition development. While it is desirable that children entering school recognize their alphabet this is not a realistic assumption. Teachers must find time to work individually with those students who do not have this skill finely honed.

4. *Upper and lower case letters should be introduced independently.* This is very essential for students who enter school with a deficit in alphabet recognition. Since the students are attempting to assimilate the sounds of the letters while recognizing their shapes, showing them both cases would only confuse them and result in low self-esteem regarding learning.

5. *Encourage initial invented spelling.* When children begin their initial writing assignments, they do not know all of the rules for spelling. Allowing students to write words as they believe they sound will heighten their phonemic awareness and understanding of spelling patters.

6. *Rhymes assist spelling.* When rhymes are utilized in lessons, it has been demonstrated that regular spelling patterns and their phonic importance have been acquired quickly. Later, encourage the

students to spell words correctly because there is a direct correlation between proper spelling and reading ability.

7. *Articulation of isolated phonemes is advantageous.* Many reading programs eliminate and do not encourage the articulation of phonemes in isolation because most cannot be pronounced without vowels. This decision often produces confused students. Research has shown that articulation of phonemes in isolation is advantageous.

8. *Reading programs should contain blending instructions.* Since students often have difficulty identifying the phonemes contained in a given word, the reading program selected should contain explicit blending instructions.

9. *Rules and generalizations are useful.* While there is no substitute for direct guided practice, it is often helpful to provide rules and generalizations for certain spelling and decoding patterns. The rules for phonics are usually valuable initially, but are inefficient once the student has begun to read.

Reflections Regarding Reading Texts

Teachers have or will be chosen to serve on the textbook committee for their particular grade level or subject. It is important that the textbook selected for several years' use be chosen not only for its subject accuracy, but for its ability to be read and comprehended by the students being instructed. How many times have textbooks been chosen because of a sleek "dog and pony" presentation by the vendor or the colorful illustrations and graphics and found to be ineffectual for instruction? The following criteria should be examined before the final textbook selection is determined (Adams, 1990):

1. *Oral reading should be easy.* Students should have a textbook which is can be easily   read with 90% to 95% accuracy. This will maximize achievement in the class and will encourage oral reading. Students in secondary school would volunteer for oral reading assignments more readily if the text is found easy to read.

2. *Textbook should correlate with grade level.* It is important to have the reading level of the students being taught represented in the text book. Many times in the secondary school environment the textbooks are written using vocabulary which does not coincide with the students' reading ability. A good example of this are the textbooks in science. If the student experiences difficulty in reading the material of a given text, he will just refuse to comply with the request. Additionally, if the explanations are too collegiate, the student will not understand how to master the given skill being presented.

3. *Textbook contains activities for skill reinforcement.* The textbook should contain exercises which will reinforce a particular skill or information being presented. These should include some which promote higher order thinking skills through inference and questioning.

Salient Strategies for Reading Instruction

Previous information in this chapter has been of a theoretical nature, now it is time to present pragmatic strategies to apply in the classroom. The strategies will be classified according to their ability to reinforce a given developmental reading stage. The information would be presented to the student at the proper developmental stage for assimilation (i.e. would not have the student searching for story inferences until he has reached the comprehension developmental stage).

1. *Phonemic awareness*
    a. Concepts to be included
    (1) Rhymes
    (2) Alliteration
    (3) Syllable counting
    (4) Phoneme Segmentation and deletion
    (5) Phoneme analysis and synthesis

    b. *Choral Word Blending*
    (1) Using this activity the teacher makes a game of sounding words with the students.
    (2) The teacher uses a hand puppet to guide the practice. The children will repeat the sounds given by the puppet.

(3)   The teacher says the initial consonant first. followed by the remainder of the word. (Example: When saying the word "cow" , the "c" is first pronounced followed by the "ow".

(4)   This activity may be used in segmentation practice. For fun, have the puppet miss some of the sounds and have the students correct him.

c.   *Rhyming Song*

(1)   This song is sung to the tune of "Old Mac Donald Had A Farm."

(2)   The teacher thinks of three words which begin with the same consonant (i.e. cow, cat, cane) and sings, "What's the sound that starts these words: *cow, cat, and cane?"*

(3)   The students respond: *"/C/* is the sound that starts these words: *cow, cat, and cane.* With a */c/ /c/* here and a */c/ /c/* there, here a /c/ there a /c/, everywhere a /c/ /C/ is the sound that starts these words: cow, cat, and cane.

2.   *Print awareness*

a.   Concepts to be included:

(1)   Environmental punt

(2)   Labeling

(3)   Punctuation marks

(4)   Concept of title, author

(5)   Title page

(6)   Table of Contents

(7)   Left to right sweeps

(8)   Italics, bold, underline

3.   Alphabetic awareness

a.   Concepts to be included

(1)   Recognition of upper and lower case letters

(2)   Alphabetical order

(3)   Differences and similarities in letter sound

(4)   Phonics instruction

4.   Orthographic awareness

a.   Concepts to be included

(1)   Phonograms

(2)   Spelling patterns

(3)   Phonic instruction

(4)   Identifying word families

(5)   Letter/sound mapping

(6)   Reading sight words

(7)   Decoding skills

5   *Reading Comprehension*

    a.   Concepts to be included

    (1)   Guided reading

    (2)   Connected text

    (3)   Story discussion

    (4)   Fact/opinion

    (5)   Inference

    (6)   Prediction /foreshadowing

    (7)   Application

    (8)   Synthesis

    (9)   Main idea

    (10)   Outlining

    (11)   Details

6.   *Reading Practice*

    a.   Concepts to be included

    (1)   Reading aloud

    (2)   Shared reading

    (3)   Teacher reading

    (4)   Paired reading

    (5)   Tape assisted reading

    (6)   Guided reading

    (7)   Independent reading

Summary

Reading is a cumulative learning process which lack of mastery in a given fundamental developmental stage will predictably hinder the students progress in the succeeding stage. The proclamation of the Roman poet Horace (1996, p.347) should be the mission statement of every teacher, "He has gained every point... by delighting the reader at the same time as instructing him." It is the responsibility of educators to design motivational and creative strategies for reading instruction which are both utilitarian and interesting. The strategies presented in this chapter should serve as a catalyst for developing additional ones which will challenge at-risk students in every grade.

References

Adam, M. J. (1990). Beginning to Read: Thinking and learning about print. Cambridge, MA: MIT Press.

Bohle, B. (Ed.). (1986). The home book of American quotations. New York, NY: Gramercy.

Hunter, P. (1997, October). A balanced approach to Reading. Paper presented at the Houston Independent School District's Principal's training meeting. Houston, TX.

Kaplan, Justin. (Ed.). (1992). Bartlet's familiar quotations. Boston: Little, Brown, and Co.

Partington. A. (Ed.). (1996). The Oxford dictionary of quotations. New York, NY: Oxford University Press.

Simpson, J. B. (1992). Webster's II new riverside desk quotations. Boston: Houghton Mifflin Co.

Texas Education Agency. (1998). A companion to beginning reading instruction. Austin, TX: Texas Center for Educational Research.

Texas Education Agency. (1997). Components and features of a research-based reading program. Austin, TX: Texas Center for Educational Research.

MELLEN STUDIES IN EDUCATION